Clive Roots

Tropical Birds

illustrated by John Rignall

Hamlyn Paperbacks

FOREWORD

There are so many birds in the equatorial regions, where they are favoured with an equable climate throughout the year and an abundance of food at all times in most areas, that it would be impossible to describe representatives of all the groups in addition to providing other information, without producing an unbalanced book. No attempt has therefore been made to do this, and my aim has merely been to give readers an insight into the tropical environment itself, together with information of a practical nature on the characteristic birds.

Unfortunately there are very few places in the tropics where the native birds are completely free from harassment by man, so I have taken a look at the association of birds and mankind, particularly how civilized man has harvested them and their products for his own ends. This, together with the often foolhardy introduction of exotic birds and mammals into the tropical birds' habitat, plus the reduction of their swamps, forests and grasslands, has resulted in many unique species becoming increasingly rare. Some have even been exterminated already; but fortunately in recent years there has been a heartening upsurge in conservation of wildlife.

The tropical jungles have always been my first love and it would have been easy to dwell solely upon the bird life there. Equal space has been given, however, to the other major bird habitats – the grasslands, wetlands and mountains – plus the bird life of the towns which has sprung up in fairly recent years in what was of course bird habitat originally. After reading this book I am sure you will agree that it is not solely the abundance or variety of birds that make the tropics the most interesting bird region in the world.

C.R.

Published by Hamlyn Paperbacks,
The Hamlyn Publishing Group Ltd,
Astronaut House, Feltham, Middlesex, England
In association with Sun Books Pty Ltd. Melbourne

Copyright © The Hamlyn Publishing Group Limited 1971
Reprinted 1982
ISBN 0 600 38606 6
Photoset by BAS Printers Limited, Wallop, Hampshire
Colour separations by Schwitter Limited, Zurich
Printed in Spain by Mateu Cromo, Madrid

CONTENTS

4	Introduction
8	Lowland forests
32	Grasslands
52	Rivers, lakes and marshes
74	Mountains
82	Tropical islands
82	Borneo
84	Galapagos
86	New Guinea
88	West Indies
90	Philippines
92	Indian Ocean
94	Towns
102	Cultivations
108	Visitors to the tropics
112	Tropical birds and man
142	Tropical birds and other animals
146	Birds in danger
156	Books to read
156	Places to visit
157	Index

AN INTRODUCTION TO TROPICAL BIRDS

Around the centre of the earth, 2,400 kilometres (1,500 miles) on either side of the Equator, lie the tropics, where the almost vertical sun produces intense heat, except on the mountains where snow may persist throughout the year. In the New World and Asia vast forests predominate. In Africa the broad central wedge of forest is enclosed on three sides by extensive grasslands and desert scrub; while in Australia the northern coastal forests are bordered by a wider band of grassland which extends into arid scrub and then desert.

Except for a few mountain species the resident birds of the

The zoogeographical regions

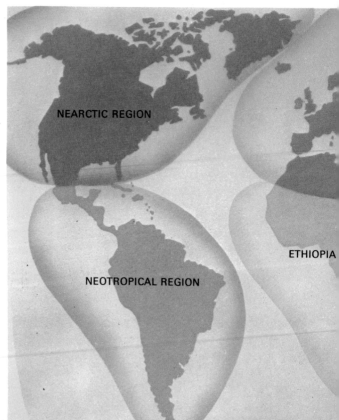

tropics are not forced by inclement weather conditions to migrate to more hospitable regions. Their migrations, when these are necessary, are associated with the search for food, and are usually fairly local and more often in the grassland areas. During part of the year their numbers are swelled by the migrants that travel south, and in fewer cases north, to escape the harsh winters of the temperate regions.

The tropics encompass four major zoogeographic zones – the Neotropical, Ethiopian, Oriental and Australasian – each with a characteristic bird population. Within these zones the geographical distribution is determined by such factors as the climate and its effect on the land, related to the conditions for which birds have become adapted. Tropical birds are more diverse than any others, and many groups are restricted

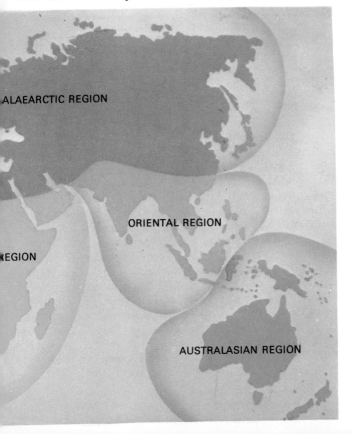

ALAEARCTIC REGION

ORIENTAL REGION

REGION

AUSTRALASIAN REGION

Akaipolaau

Akialoa

Adaptive radiation among honeycreepers

to the equatorial regions, where there is a greater abundance of food in all areas except the most arid.

Natural selection has brought about the evolution of these specialized forms. Birds evolved from reptiles and, like all other animals, the variations they underwent during this process assisted their chances of survival, or otherwise. Over a long period the variations that improved their means of gathering food, escaping from their enemies and surviving natural disasters tended to persist, and those of little use to the bird were eliminated. As birds evolved they became adapted for living wherever the conditions were favourable. In fact wherever food was available birds colonized the habitat and slowly became modified for existence there. Many unrelated, and widely separated, birds evolved on similar lines as a result of adaptation to the same mode of life. Consequently similar habitats throughout the tropics are occupied by unrelated birds that resemble each other superficially. For example, the tropical American honeycreepers, which are dependent upon flowers and small insects for survival, are

Iiwi

Palila

Akapa

paralleled in Africa by the sunbirds and in Australia by the honeyeaters, and are all very similar. This is known as convergence, and is in contrast to the adaptive radiation that occurs in isolated populations of a single species.

Adaptive radiation is particularly noticeable in insular communities, where there has been divergence in the characters of related birds to enable them to exploit all types of habitat in the absence of competition from other birds. The honeycreepers of the Hawaiian islands are a very good example of adaptive radiation. With no competitors for food, these small birds, which are similar in form and habit but dissimilar in colour and bill shape, have evolved into seed-eaters, nectar-feeders and insectivorous birds. The bills of the seed-eaters are so large that they have been named Parrot-billed Honeycreepers, while the most beautiful species could easily be mistaken for Asiatic sunbirds. These honeycreepers are restricted to the Hawaiian islands, and in some cases are endemic to a single island. Almost a quarter of the known species are now extinct, mainly owing to the loss of their habitat to man and predation by introduced animals.

THE BIRDS OF THE LOWLAND FORESTS

There are three main types of lowland forest in the tropics, the rain, seasonal or monsoon, and secondary; the last is due in almost all instances to man's interference. Rain forest covers the largest area, blanketing vast regions of America, Africa, Indonesia, South East Asia and, to a lesser extent, northern Australia. Often known as the primaeval or equatorial forest, it is the 'Jungle' of films and novels. It is evergreen, although not in the sense that some temperate forests are. The trees lose their leaves intermittently throughout the year and at all times the overall impression when flying over these regions is of a dense green carpet, relieved occasionally by a clearing or river. Within this major habitat the forest clearings also form a niche of their own, with many characteristic insectivorous birds flying out to catch passing insects from the trees bordering the clearings.

After a few years forest clearings are usually left fallow as man moves on. Trees from the neighbouring forest invade these areas, but the depleted soil favours the growth of shrubs and climbing plants, as most of its growing power will have been leached by the torrential rains after the loss of its

(*Left*) Coppersmith Barbet (*top*) and Wire-tailed Manakin;
(*above*) Blue-winged Leafbird (*left*) and Blue Fairy
Flycatcher

protective mantle of leaves. The result is a tangled mass of
vegetation, with an abundance of berries and insect life, and
its characteristic fauna. Secondary forest is particularly
evident in parts of tropical Asia.

Where there is a definite seasonal rainfall the forests take
on a completely different aspect. The largest area of this type
of forest occurs in South East Asia in the monsoon belt, and
there are smaller areas in central Africa and South America.
This forest is far more deciduous than the rain forest and, even
in areas where the wet season is extended, many trees shed
all their leaves during the short dry season. This seasonal
leaf loss allows the light to penetrate to the forest floor,
unheard of in the rain forest, and the undergrowth is dense.
The rainfall varies considerably in the monsoon forests. In
the wettest parts of Burma the rainy season from May to
October may produce 755 centimetres (250 inches) of rain. In
the drier regions deciduous teak is the dominant tree species
in the forests, and thick clumps of bamboo are common,
especially on the hillsides.

A fourth type of vegetation – the mangrove 'forest' – is
restricted to the estuaries and coastal mudflats where the sea

and silt-carrying rivers mingle. The mangroves form a tangled mass of prop roots and evergreen vegetation, trapping silt until eventually the accumulation of debris is able to support other trees and shrubs.

Over the years the forest-dwelling birds have become adapted to make full use of their habitat, with modifications that have improved their chances of finding food, mates, nesting sites and all the other daily activities that are necessary for survival. The feet of many arboreal species are adapted to give them a better grip when perching, climbing or feeding. The parrots, for instance, have zygodactylous feet, with two toes pointing forwards and two backwards, which allows them to hold food with their feet. They are capable climbers and can also use their heavy bills as an extra foot. The fruit pigeons have thick fleshy legs with wide toes and

Head and foot of African Grey Parrot

Head and foot of Violet Plantain-eater

Head and foot of Woodhewer

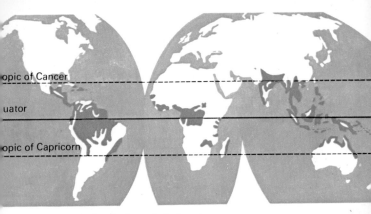

uator

The worldwide distribution of rain forest areas.

large soles and seldom venture to the ground, which applies equally to birds in which flight is highly developed – for instance, the hummingbirds – and in which the feet are ridiculously small in proportion to their size.

The beaks of the arboreal species are modified to allow them to feed upon forest produce: fruit and berries, nuts, nectar from flowers, even the flowers themselves, and insects. The imperial fruit pigeons (*Ducula* spp.) of Indonesia and the Pacific islands have weak bills but very flexible mandibles, and an enormous gape. They are able to swallow large drupes complete with stones which they later eject. The green pigeons (*Treron* spp.) differ in having muscular gizzards and are able to digest the seeds of wild figs and other fruits. The members of the parrot family have powerful, sharp bills, and the larger species can feed on the kernels of the hardest shelled nuts. The Black Palm Cockatoos (*Probosciger aterrimus*) of Australia and New Guinea have large compressed beaks with which they are able to crush palm nuts. One group of parrots, the Lorinae, have smaller bills with highly modified brush-tipped tongues which allow them to gather pollen and nectar from tree flowers. The hummingbirds are also adapted for such a diet but they hover in front of a flower and insert their protractile tongue into the mouth of the corolla. If this is exceptionally long they can even pierce the side of the corolla to reach the nectar.

11

Birds dependent upon tree trunks, and therefore denizens of the rain and monsoon forests, are well represented there compared with the temperate woodlands. The forests of Colombia, for instance, shelter thirty-five of the known 208 species of woodpeckers, and twenty-six species of woodcreepers. There are also several species of barbets, although the forests of South East Asia are their stronghold. The woodpeckers (Picidae) are the most highly adapted for life on the tree trunks and have distinctive climbing and feeding habits. Their extremely long and mobile tongues, the hard tips of which may be edged with barbs, can be coated with mucus for catching ants and termites, or can be used to stab larger insects. The true woodpeckers, such as the Great Slaty Woodpecker (*Mulleripicus pulverulentus*) of Malaya, have hard, chisel-like bills with which they drill their nest holes, and bristles around their nostrils to prevent wood-dust from entering their lungs. Large heads and strong neck

Yellow-naped Woodpecker (*top*) and the diminutive African Piculet at its hole.

12

The extraordinarily long tongue of a woodpecker is capable of an extreme degree of protrusion because of the great length of the supporting bones coiled inside the skull.

muscles power their bills, and to aid climbing they have stiffened tails and short strong feet equipped with very sharp claws. The woodcreepers (Dendrocolaptidae) are a tropical American family, and have the stiffened tails of the true woodpeckers but have weak bills and cannot drill holes. Some have long, curved beaks, but a slightly hooked though otherwise straight bill is characteristic of most of them. The Red-billed Scythebill (*Campyloramphus trochilirostris*) is only 23 centimetres (9 inches) long, yet has a bill 6 centimetres ($2\frac{1}{2}$ inches) long. Unlike the woodpeckers they build a nest of leaves in hollow stumps and sometimes in holes abandoned by other birds.

The barbets (Capitonidae) are primarily forest birds, where they are sedentary, seldom moving far through the tree tops in search of insects and fruit. With heavy, sharp-tipped beaks they drill their own nest holes in rotting wood; and their name is derived from the feather tufts around the nostrils. These tufts are usually black, but in the Fire-tufted Barbet (*Psilopogon pyrolophus*) of South East Asia are red. Many forest birds depend upon the holes made by woodpeckers and barbets for their nesting sites, sometimes even usurping the rightful owners. Small holes are used by starlings and grackles, and larges ones by toucans.

The toucans (Ramphastidae) of the New World tropical forests must be the most bizarre of all birds, yet the reason they have such large bills is still unknown. It has been suggested that their length of bill allows them to reach fruits on thin, outlying branches that would not bear their weight, but a slender bill would have served as well for this purpose as one almost 6 centimetres ($2\frac{1}{2}$ inches) wide. It has also been suggested that their beaks would be useful to intimidate the rightful owners when the toucans were robbing other birds' nests. Or they may have been evolved to protect their own nests when these were threatened; but this seems hardly likely as many toucans abandon their nest holes the moment they are disturbed. The bill markings, often highly coloured, apparently act as social signals and prevent confusion among the many species.

Their bills are certainly not as cumbersome or heavy as they appear, however. The hard, horny outer shell covers a network of bony fibres, and combines lightness with strength; with the serrated edges or pincer-like tip they can easily draw blood from the hand. To fit their bills they have tongues up

Toco Toucan (*top*) and Sulphur Toucan

to 15 centimetres (6 inches) long in the largest species, but they cannot swallow food items placed in the tip of the bill. Everything has to be thrown into the air and caught in the base of the bill before it can be swallowed.

In the Old World they are replaced by the hornbills (Bucerotidae), although they are not related to them – an example of the convergence mentioned on page 6. Most of the hornbills are tropical forest-dwellers living upon fruits and invertebrates like the toucans, but when small birds fly within reach of their bills they catch and eat those also. The forest species generally have a casque at the base of the upper mandible, and until fairly recently the Chinese carved ornaments from the casque of the Helmeted Hornbill (*Rhinoplax vigil*), one of the largest species. It is the only species to suffer from the trade in 'hornbill ivory' as its casque provides a small solid block of horn, whereas the others are cellular like the toucans' bills. Only a few of these ornaments exist in museum collections and they are valued more highly than gold or jade carvings.

Although female hornbills have smaller bills and less

Laminated Toucan (*top*) and Great Hornbill

prominent casques than the males, both sexes of most species have exactly the same plumage coloration and pattern, which also applies to the toucans. Where differences exist, and in many birds they are strikingly obvious, it is known as sexual dimorphism, and can take the form of differences in size or of plumage. In the tropics, particularly in the forests, there are many examples of plumage differences between the male and female birds of the same species. Sexual dimorphism has been evolved to avoid hybridization among closely related species, and the characters of the males reduce the chances of a female choosing an 'unsuitable' mate. The males of some insular species, which are separated from closely related species, may lose these differentiating features or characters as it is impossible for the females to make a mistake when seeking a mate. Within species, especially polygamous ones, there is competition for mates and as only the secondary sexual characters of the males are involved (those characters peculiar to them that determine their difference in appearance) there has been an increase in sexual dimorphism.

The polygamous arena display males are highly coloured,

Sexual dimorphism in Flame Dove (*above*) and Eclectus Parrot

and do not assist in the task of incubating the eggs or rearing the young as this would draw attention to the nest. The height of vivid coloration is achieved by the male cocks of the rock (*Rupicola* spp.), which are either deep scarlet, orange or apricot. In the Coraciiformes – kingfishers, rollers, motmots, for example – the parrots (Psittacidae) and most of the pigeons (Columbidae), plumage dimorphism is absent, and both sexes of most species are highly coloured. One notable exception is the Flame Dove (*Ptilinopus victor*) of Fiji, the males of which are reddish-orange with an olive head, and the females dark green with a yellowish head. Another is the Eclectus Parrot (*Lorius roratus*) of Indonesia which is one of the most striking examples of sexual dimorphism among birds; both sexes are brightly coloured, but with a different colour scheme, the male being green whereas the female is red and blue.

Where dimorphism is not related to sex it is known as polymorphism, when there may exist a number of colour forms within an interbreeding population. Among tropical forest birds the most notable example is the Many-coloured Bush Shrike (*Chlorophoneus multicolor*) of the central African

Male King Bird of Paradise displaying to female

forests. There are five colour forms or 'morphs', all differing in the coloration of their underparts, which may be crimson, black, pink, yellow or buff.

Small animals and vegetable matter form the bulk of the diet of most tropical forest birds. The animal food is generally termed 'insects' but can include worms, snails, young lizards, geckos and many other forms of life. Most insectivorous species eat whatever comes their way, but a few have a more specialized food intake and feeding methods. The Shovel-billed Kingfisher (*Clytoceyx rex*) of New Guinea has a large blunt beak which is often caked with mud, and H. Hamlin, who has observed this species in the wild state, says that it thrusts its beak into the soft soil of the forest floor searching for something. Apparently it was looking for earthworms, as other observers have seen birds pulling worms from the soil, and examination of their stomach contents has also revealed worms. The Hook-billed Kingfisher (*Melidora macrorhina*) of the same country is also a forest bird with similar ground feeding habits, but it is thought to rely mainly upon the

Some typical fruit- and insect-eating species : Imperial Fruit Pigeon (*top*) and Rainbow Lorikeet ;

insects that it unearths from the loose soil. Kingfishers are usually associated with water, but like the above species there are many that dwell in the forests many miles from the nearest water, and even if water were near at hand, they would not dream of diving for fish. They behave in the manner of the bee-eaters (Meropidae), flying from a favourite perch to snatch a passing insect, and returning to the same branch to beat their prey before swallowing it.

The Oilbird (*Steatornis caripensis*) of the northern South American forests must have the most specialized feeding habits of the frugivorous birds, as it feeds solely on the fruits of certain palms, which have a very high oil content but are low in protein. Oilbirds are nocturnal; they probably locate ripe palm fruits by sight but have developed a highly specialized echo-location technique which enables them to manoeuvre their way out of the caves where they roost and nest. Due to the low protein content of the palm nuts the young Oilbirds spend up to four months in their nests, which are always built in the deepest caves. They grow very fat,

Royal Flycatcher (*top left*), Paradise Jacamar (*top right*) and Red-eyed Vireo

Birds flocking to fruiting fig tree : (*left to right*) Bushy-crested Hornbill, Large Green Pigeon, Cinnamon-headed Green Pigeon and Malay Lorikeet

but put on flesh and feathers slowly.

With the exception of the Oilbird it is doubtful if any birds are entirely frugivorous in their feeding habits. Other fruit-eating species such as the touracos (Musophagidae) include invertebrates in their diet, especially when rearing their young, and many are known to make use of 'salt licks' and other natural mineral deposits to provide the mineral salts that are essential to all but the most modified birds.

Most frugivorous forest birds make local migrations through the tree tops in search of fruiting or flowering trees. The naturalist and author Williame Beebe once spent many hours sitting quietly under a fruiting wild cinnamon tree in the Brazilian jungle in Pará State, observing the number of birds that visited it. He positively identified seventy-six species and saw at least thirty-three others new to him. During one

vigil of two hours' duration he counted over 400 birds in the tree, most of them feeding on the berries. An interesting feature was that many insectivorous birds, including fly-catchers, ate the berries as avidly as the manakins, tanagers and toucans.

In South East Asia trees with particularly attractive flowers, fruits or berries are visited by flocks of fruit pigeons, horn-bills, fairy bluebirds and lories. On the forest floor the berries that are dropped attract pheasants, peafowl and partridges, in addition to many mammals. The insectivorous species of the Malaysian forests benefit from group hunting. Bands of insect-seeking birds move rapidly through the trees and undergrowth and make a mass attack upon the insects disturbed by their twittering and fluttering. Except when the nuthatches, drongos, babblers, flycatchers and warblers co-operate in the business of finding food, they are not sociable in their habits.

In South America some ground-dwelling insectivorous forest birds follow the columns of ants, and benefit from the insects that are driven out of hiding in their efforts to escape.

Unlike the layers of vegetation in the temperate forests where herbs, shrubs and trees are clearly defined, the primaeval rain forests of South America present a complex facade of leafy canopies mounted upon canopies, like layers of clouds, with little beneath them. The sun cannot penetrate the thick layer of leaves, and the dank compost heap of sodden leaf mould below is hardly encouraging to plant life. A few weedy saplings sprout here and there, but the vegetation scarcely warrants the name of undergrowth. The lower canopy rises to about 18 metres (60 feet) high, and consists of mature smaller species, and a few young specimens of the forest giants that will eventually reach a height of 45 metres (150 feet). In South America there are still more than 2,500,000 square kilometres (1,000,000 square miles) of this evergreen forest, and its bird populations are well defined.

High above the canopy soar the huge Harpy Eagles (*Harpia harpya*), looking mainly for mammalian prey, and the graceful Swallow-tailed Kite (*Elanoides forficatus*) and the Black and White Hawk Eagle (*Spizastur melaneleucus*). Vultures – the King (*Sarcorhamphus papa*) and Turkey (*Cathartes aura*) species – also quarter the forest. In the forest canopy itself there is a large resident population of birds, including cotingas, jays, parrots and toucans, together with flocks of the smaller tanagers and honeycreepers, all continually moving through the tree tops in search of food. Barbets (Capitonidae) also live in the tree tops although some species venture down to the lower levels of the trunks in search of insects. A number of fowl-like birds, the curassows and guans of the family Cracidae, also live in the canopy, and nest there too, but bring their precocial young down to the ground as soon as they hatch. They feed on the ground in the manner of the pheasants, but roost at night in the trees away from the terrestrial predators.

In the sparse undergrowth live the manakins (Pipridae), brightly coloured sparrow-sized birds that pluck small berries from the branches in flight. They frequently 'migrate' to the canopy to feed from fruiting trees.

Vertical zonation of a rain forest (not drawn to scale).

Canopy

Blue-grey Tanager

Black-necked Red Cotinga

Intermediate

Scythebill

Toucan Barbet

Forest floor

Tinamou

Streak-chested Antpitta

At ground level in the forests live the quail doves, leaf-scrapers, tinamous and antbirds. The tinamous (Tinamidae) are the only purely terrestrial species, and nest on the ground. Some of them even roost on the ground, a rather precarious business at night when so many predators are on the prowl. All of these birds are made even more inconspicuous by their nondescript colouring. Most of the 223 species of antbirds (Formicarlidae), for example the ant-thrushes, anti-pittas and ant-shrikes, and the tinamous, are clad in shades of brown, rufous, grey and black, but the result is handsome if not colourful.

Throughout the world the tropical forest floor is the home of many species of birds, but most of them are skulkers and are seldom seen. The general impression after a walk through the forest is of a distinct lack of bird life, and only when the birdwatcher remains perfectly still for some time do the birds appear. Until 1936 it was thought that peafowl (*Pavo* spp.) were not represented in Africa, but in that year the ornithological world was amazed by the discovery in the central African forests of the Congo Peafowl (*Afropavo*

African Peacock

24

congensis). Although small 'new' birds are still occasionally discovered, it is remarkable that such a large bird should have remained unknown until recent years.

The Congo Peacock is a colourful bird, and in contrast with the New World there are many other highly coloured terrestrial species in the tropical forests of the Old World. Pittas and some species of partridges and pheasants replace the antthrushes and tinamous, and several of them warrant the title of the world's most beautiful bird. The Garnet Pitta (*Pitta granatina*) of the Malay peninsula and Indonesia is one of the most attractive species, and has deep red underparts and head, and upperparts of several shades of violet and blue. The Crested Fireback Pheasant (*Lophura ignita*), Malay Peacock Pheasant (*Polyplectron malacense*) and the Crested Green Wood Partridge (*Rollulus roulroul*) have the same distribution as the Garnet Pitta and are all highly coloured. Powerful legs and toes are characteristic of many of the terrestrial forest birds, and are an adaptation for scratching among the leaf mould for

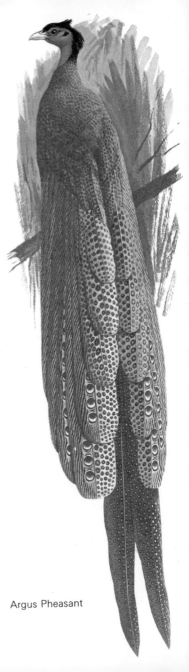

Argus Pheasant

worms, insects and their larvae, and fallen berries and seeds.

The brilliant and conspicuous coloration of some birds – phaneric coloration – has been evolved to promote a number of biological functions, including warning, threat and recognition; and during evolution some movements have also become specialized and function as social communication signals. These may be used to indicate aggression or submission, as greetings or during courtship, and for other reasons. The exchanges of signals between potential mates may be visual in the case of courtship display, or auditory in the case of singing. Birds living in thick forest usually have loud and continuous songs with which they attract their mates. In some forest species elaborate courtship displays have been evolved, particularly in the manakins, the birds of paradise, bowerbirds and the cocks of the rock. Unlike the pair relationship of most birds which may last for several weeks or even longer, these birds have only a temporary pair bond, individuals of the opposite sex meeting at these 'lek' displays for mating. Lek is now the accepted name given to all displays where the males gather in small areas and display to one or more females which mate with the dominant male.

Most of the males of the lek species are brightly coloured and have unusual adornments, some even having sound-making adaptations to attract females. The Gould's Manakin (*Manacus vitellinus*), for instance, has thickened wing quills with which it makes a snapping sound.

The areas in which the lek birds display, often the same spot year after year, are known as courts. For some species they may be on the ground, for others a tree-top display has been evolved. The cocks of the rock (*Rupicola* spp.) have brilliant red or orange plumage and striking crests, which help young females without breeding experience to identify them. Many adjacent display arenas may be formed in a relatively small area of forest, and these are cleared of all debris before the birds display. The Magnificent Bird of Paradise (*Diphyllodes magnificus*) displays on a low branch over a cleared arena which may be up to 5 metres (15 feet) in diameter. All leaves and twigs are removed, and stronger saplings are continually denuded of leaves until they die. 'Ring-barking' small saplings to kill them has also been

Lek display of male cocks of the rock

witnessed. Males of the Greater Bird of Paradise (*Paradisaea apoda*) display in the tree tops, and as many as twenty males may congregate to attract with their noise and colour the females which are free to select their own mates.

The females of the lek species are less conspicuous than the males and are responsible for the nesting chores to ensure that attention is not drawn to the nest. This brief association of birds of opposite sexes also occurs in other species, but in a different manner. The hen Wagler's or Chestnut-headed Oropendola (*Zarhynchus wagleri*), for example, builds her nest first and then associates with a male, afterwards completing the incubation and chick rearing with no help from him. Nest building is, of course, a specialized part of a bird's reproductive cycle and the many methods at present in use have been evolved over a long period. The raising of a family is also a precarious business, as there are far more predators seeking birds' nests in the tropical forests than in any other region in the world. Monkeys, squirrels, bushbabies, tree shrews, snakes, lizards, carnivorous and omnivorous birds all strive to vary their diet with eggs or nestlings. Evolution has fortunately adapted the nesting behaviour of birds to overcome these obstacles, and one of their means of doing this is to site their nests in the most inaccessible places. The oropendolas (Icteridae), for instance, suspend their pendulous nests on the outermost branches of giant forest trees, over 30 metres (100 feet) above ground. They also build their nests close to the nests of aggressive wasps, and this combination of employing two nest-protective devices is common to several other species. The malimbus or forest weavers (*Malimbus* spp.) weave their tough nests on branches overhanging water, and frequently in association with wasps. So there is definite proof that some birds purposely nest close to the nests of dangerous insects to benefit from the protection that these undoubtedly afford. In South America some tanagers nest close to the aggressive Kiskadees (*Pitangus sulphuratus*). Other species form an even closer association with insects and nest within their nests. In fact wherever the arboreal nests of termites and ants occur in the tropics they are used by

Green Oropendolas at their nests

kingfishers, woodpeckers, parrots, jacamars and trogons.

Nest sanitation is also important. Firstly from the hygiene point of view; secondly to protect the nest from predators who may become aware of its existence because of the accumulation of droppings underneath or around it. The nidicolous young of most tree nesters are particularly vulnerable when in the nest and as they begin to fly, and egg shells beneath the nest could prove disastrous. Soon after the eggs have hatched it is usual for the female to carry away the egg shells, and in species which construct fine downy nests, or delicately woven ones, the nestlings' droppings are either swallowed or carried some distance from the nest by the parents.

Fledgelings in open nests are protected from the elements during the day by the outspread wings and tails of the adult birds, and are of course brooded at night. The young of hole-nesting birds are certainly less vulnerable to most predators, and the hornbills have evolved unique nesting habits which protect them from all but the most persistent and strong-clawed carnivorous animals. A hole up to 30 metres (100 feet) above ground level is chosen for the nesting site and the female is sealed into this by the male. A mixture of mud, saliva and vegetable matter is used, and the female assists in completing the task from inside. The mixture sets like cement and with only a narrow slit remaining of the original entrance, the male hornbill tirelessly feeds the imprisoned hen for the full incubation and rearing period which may last for three months. When the fledgelings are quite large the hens of some species break their way out, seal up the nest again and help the male to feed them. Nest sanitation is overcome by voiding the droppings out through the narrow opening, but this has its drawbacks as the hunting tribes of South East Asia and Indonesia are able to tell from the growth of seeds at the base of the tree when the young are mature enough to be collected. Nest holes of the Silvery-cheeked Hornbill (*Bycanistes brevis*) of Africa have been found to contain insect larvae and beetles, which no doubt are important in maintaining the cleanliness of the nest.

Male Rhinoceros Hornbill feeding 'imprisoned' mate

BIRDS OF THE TROPICAL GRASSLANDS

For the purpose of this book 'grasslands' is a loose name for all forms of open country from the savannah woodland to the deserts where grass is absent, or at most very sparse. Between the true grasslands, where trees are virtually absent, and the forests there are transitional zones where the dominant vegetation is grass with a few scattered trees. This is the savannah woodland or parkland and in some areas there may even be remnants of forest within this grassland. These intermediate grass and tree zones are very irregular, however, and in some places are practically non-existent, the forest suddenly giving way to grassland. In other areas the rainfall may be as high as in the forests, yet trees do not claim the land; this is mainly owing to the action of man in burning the grass periodically to improve the grazing, and to the grazing animals themselves. Where the rainfall is exceptionally high, as in parts of West Africa for example, the grasses may grow up to 3 metres (10 feet) tall, but in other parts of Africa

Typical grassland birds: (*left to right*) Crowned Crane, Vulturine Guineafowl, Harlequin Quail, Kori Bustard and Red-necked Spurfowl

the poor soil and lack of rain for most of the year result in sparse grassland, except when the rains occur. In Africa the characteristic trees of this type of habitat are the acacias, and these are also found in the corresponding Australian grasslands, where eucalypts are equally abundant.

The seasonal changes in the dry savannahs are very distinct. Most birds breed to take advantage of the abundance of food towards the end of the rains for rearing their young, when grasses are seeding and insects have reached their peak in numbers. In the very dry regions grass forms a sparse cover to the stony or sandy soil, and the low annual rainfall does little to relieve the monotony. Deciduous thorn bushland appears in places, and it is a land of modifications to store water or to offset water loss. The plants have woody stems, and some trees store water in their swollen trunks. The Caatinga of north-eastern Brazil is one of the largest areas of tropical thorn and scrub country in the world. In other areas, particularly in Africa, the dry scrubland and sparse grassland eventually give way to the true desert, where plant life is almost non-existent, and the few birds are either insectivorous or carnivorous.

The African grasslands form the largest single area of tropical open space in the world, and occupy most of the land mass in the tropics, being almost divided by the central wedge of forest. They are the home of many terrestrial species which spend most of their time on the ground, even nesting there, and one flightless bird – the Ostrich (*Struthio camelus*). It has no alternative to using its powerful legs to carry it to a safe distance, but many of the others are strong fliers yet still prefer to run to safety. These grasslands are the stronghold of the game birds, and there are thirty-three members of the pheasant family (Phasianidae) resident in East Africa alone. Spurfowl, guineafowl, partridges and francolins abound, in addition to eleven species of bustards and many crakes, coursers and pratincoles.

Ostriches are found throughout the plains and thorn scrub country, except, of course, in the settled areas. Their powerful limbs and excellent vision make them difficult to catch in their open habitat, even by lions. In common with the other grassland ratites (birds that lack the keel on the sternum or breastbone) – the Emu of Australia and the rheas of South America – the cock Ostrich incubates the eggs, although the hens relieve him for part of the day. The incubation period is six weeks, and the male bird is polygamous and may have five hens in his entourage, all laying in the same nest. There is insufficient food available for them in the very dry country, and they roam the plains in search of the vegetable matter which forms their food, and from which it is assumed that they derive sufficient moisture. Although the earliest known birds could only glide, it is now generally believed that flightlessness in the Ostrich is secondary, and that they evolved their powerful legs, large size and terrestrial habits perhaps somewhere other than Africa, where there is a large species population of predators not conducive to loss of flight.

The Emu (*Dromaius novaehollandiae*) is the second largest ratite and replaces the Ostrich on the Australian grasslands. It is unique in having loose, hair-like feathers, as the barbs are not hooked together.

Ostrich (Masai race) with females

No birds can live where there is neither food nor water, yet surprisingly many can thrive where water is unavailable. Some of these derive all the moisture they need from insects, others from their vegetable food. Alternatively others travel long distances to find water; one species of sandgrouse (Pteroclididae), for example, has been recorded travelling over 70 miles daily to fill its crop. Others, such as the Sarus Crane (*Grus antigone*), are seldom seen far from water.

The bee-eaters (Meropidae) are not known to drink and apparently derive suffcient moisture from the insects that form their food. The mainly terrestrial bustards (Otididae), on the other hand, eat large quantities of locusts, yet obtain their fluids from vegetable matter. The Sudan Bustard (*Ardeotis arabs stieberi*), a bird of the arid plains and waterless desert in the French Sudan, is said to eat desert water melons. The Vulturine Guineafowl (*Acryllium volturinum*) is thought to be dependent upon dew for its water supplies for most of the year.

(Left to right) Cream Courser, Pintail Sandgrouse and Sarus Crane

Another adaptation for grassland living is a colour scheme that will camouflage the bird and make it less obvious to potential predators. Cryptic coloration is the name given to camouflage designed to protect animals from their enemies, and it takes two basic forms. Firstly, there is obliterative shading, where the darkest colour is on the bird's back and the lightest on the underparts, which renders it virtually invisible as the body appears as a flat surface. Many terrestrial birds of the open country, such as bustards, thicknees, button quail and francolins have this form of coloration, and associated with this is concealment by immobility and crouching. This not only helps to blend them into the background, but also reduces the shadow that would otherwise be cast. These birds are all reluctant to take flight when alarmed, and prefer to crouch motionless on the sand or stones where they are virtually invisible. Others, such as the coursers (Glareolidae), prefer to dash away at top speed.

Unlike the birds mentioned above, the lapwings and plovers have a bold colour scheme, but its effect is disruptive and it is therefore as cryptic as the others.

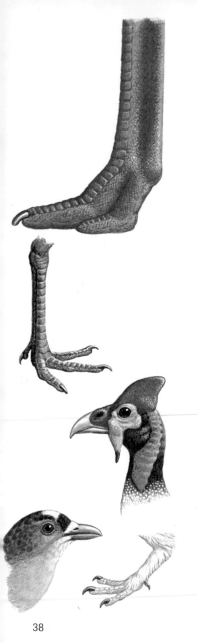

The larks (Alaudidae) have evolved to perfection to suit their habitat, and the desert larks (*Ammomanes* spp.) have plumage coloration that so closely resembles the earth in their particular localized habitats that they are reluctant to leave them. Many species live in the most arid regions and some even occur in central Arabia, where a dark race of the Desert Lark (*Ammomanes deserti annae*) lives on the black laval outcrops, and a sand-coloured race on the adjoining desert. Both remain aloof as they would be very conspicuous in the wrong area.

Adaptations that have evolved to suit a bird for terrestrial life include modifications of the feet and toes, although these are not of course restricted to birds living in the grasslands. Birds that run from their enemies have long legs, but the Secretary Bird (*Sagittarius serpentarius*) of Africa has long legs which allow it to evade venomous reptiles which form part of its diet. Four toes is the maximum number for birds, but the

(*Top to bottom*) Foot of Ostrich; foot and head of Helmeted Guineafowl; head and foot of sandgrouse

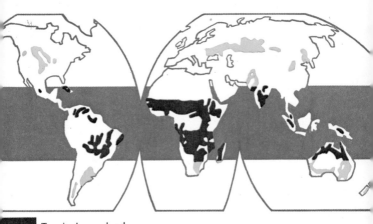

■ Tropical grassland

Principal grassland areas

walking species, as opposed to those with perching feet, have lost their power to grip objects, the hind toe has become elevated and is reduced in size, and sometimes through lack of use has been lost altogether. In some species the forward facing toes have very broad soles which aid swiftness over sandy soil, and the Ostrich shows the most extreme form of adaptation as it has only two toes, both pointing forward, which have 'cushioned' soles to prevent them sinking into sandy ground. Any lessening of contact with the ground, from four toes to three or two, aids running. The sandgrouse have their three forward-pointing toes connected by a membrane that holds them together, another adaptation for living in a sandy habitat. The Plains Wanderer (*Pedionomus torquatus*) of the Australian grasslands has a hind toe, and actually stands on its toes to get a better view of the terrain. The scratching birds – members of the pheasant family (Phasionidae) for example – have powerful legs and toes which are equipped with strong claws, and they are able to unearth food items beneath the earth surface. Their short, thick bills, with slightly longer, overhanging upper mandibles, are ideal implements for probing out insects, worms, seeds and roots.

Pennant-winged Nightjar

The grasslands are also the home of many arboreal birds which venture to the ground to feed and drink, but roost in trees and normally nest there too. Many of them are flock birds and are more migratory than the terrestrial species as they need to fly daily to a source of water. In the Australian deserts, and no doubt elsewhere, lost travellers have been able to locate water supplies by following the direction of the early morning bird flights. Wherever trees are found on the grasslands the arboreal species abound, and at least equal the purely terrestrial birds. In the South American grasslands there is a whole host of nondescript species known simply as seed-finches or seedeaters. Following the general rule that dull-plumaged birds have the best songs, the males of several species are quite melodious and are sought as cage birds. In some areas singing contests are still held, and one of the favourite species is the Variable Seedeater (*Sporophila americana*), a common bird of the grasslands bordering the great forests of northern South America. The Glossy Grassquit (*Volatina jacarina*), on the other hand, utters only a single

Scarlet-breasted Sunbird (*left*) and Green-throated Mango Hummingbird

'zeet', and jumps upwards from its perch when doing this.

The world's most attractive seed-eating birds occur in Africa and Australia, and Gouldian Finches (*Chloebia gouldiae*) and Diamond Sparrows (*Zonaeginthus guttatus*) and other species from the latter continent were in great demand as cage birds until their exportation was banned. The bishop birds, weavers and whydahs of Africa show strong sexual dimorphism with the cock birds clad in contrasting black and yellow or scarlet, with dark face masks on a yellowish body, or with elongated tails, respectively. The hens are permanently a dull, streaky brown, but during the non-breeding season most males assume a similar plumage to the hens and are virtually indistinguishable from them externally. The bishops and non-parasitic whydahs weave globular-shaped nests in long grass, which have an entrance near the top on one side. The weavers of the genus *Ploceus* construct elaborate suspended nests in reed beds or trees, which take a variety of forms and usually have a funnel-shaped entrance.

41

Hummingbirds can be found on the tropical grasslands of South America wherever there are trees and in the Old World the nectar- and insect-eating sunbirds replace them. The Green-throated Mango Hummingbird (*Anthracothorax viridigula*) is common in the savannah country of the Guianas; while in Angola the Dusky Sunbird (*Nectarinia fusca*) is resident in the very arid country, extending down into the waterless Karroo, where it is said to feed from aloe flowers. Several species of parrots also inhabit the dry thorn bush country of Africa, although they are seldom found far from a source of water. The commonest species is the Brown or Meyer's Parrot (*Poicephalus meyeri*), a tree-hole nester, whereas the Rosy-faced Lovebird (*Agapornis roseicollis*) of Angola nests in rock crevices in dry, mountainous country. Parrots are not experts in sustained flight and the Australian Ground Parrot (*Pezoporus wallicus*) has virtually lost its flying capacity in the absence of predators, and nests among grass.

In Africa many hornbills are grassland birds, and insects form the bulk of their diet. Compared with the forest species

Lilac-breasted Roller (*left*) and Red-billed Hornbill

they are rather small birds with slender bodies and curved bills, and lack the casques and colour schemes common to the others. They are less arboreal than the birds mentioned above as they feed mainly upon the ground, but they are just as dependent upon trees for nesting. Numerous eagles and smaller birds of prey frequent the open country of the tropics, far more than are found over the forests. Of the fourteen species of eagles occurring in East Africa the majority are birds of the grasslands, where they nest in large trees and sometimes use them as vantage points from which to pounce on unsuspecting animals. They are perhaps aerial birds as opposed to arboreal ones, as much of their time is spent in flight searching for food. This applies equally to the rollers (Coraciidae), those handsome masters of acrobatic flight, although most of their food is taken on the ground and they nest in tree holes. The bee-eaters (Meropidae) are even less dependent upon trees, as they nest and roost in holes in sandbanks, and spend most of the daylight hours in soaring flight catching insects on the wing.

Turquoise Parakeet (*left*) and Red Bishopbird

Apart from the multitude of small grain-eating birds, the grasslands are the home of mainly insectivorous and carnivorous birds. Many birds of prey also eat insects. The Swallow-tailed Kite (*Elanoides forficatus*) catches them on the wing and is thought to be wholly insectivorous; and even vultures have been recorded feeding on locust swarms. The Grasshopper Buzzard (*Butastur rufipennis*) relies on insects, and if there is one in the vicinity of a grass fire it will certainly be drawn to it to collect the invertebrates that are disturbed. Other birds congregate there, too, particularly the hawking Carmine Bee-eaters (*Merops rubicus*), which have also been seen riding on the backs of bustards to snap up the insects disturbed as these large birds stalk through the grass.

The wealth of lizards and snakes on the grasslands are eagerly sought as food by many birds. The only terrestrial hornbills in the world – the two ground hornbills (*Bucorvus* spp.) of the African savannahs – are carnivorous and several have been seen to tackle large lizards and

Kookaburra

snakes that would certainly have been more than a match for one bird. Reptiles are also the favourite food of the harrier eagles (Circinae) and the snake-hunting species travel many miles daily in search of their prey. Beaudouin's Harrier Eagle (*Circaetus gallicus*) which occurs in a narrow strip of country dividing the West African grasslands and the Sahara is said to eat only snakes. Their young are reared on snakes, which they swallow whole, an operation that may take several hours.

Surprisingly, several species of kingfishers also occur in the grasslands of the Old World, where they feed on many forms of animal life other than fish. Some nest in banks like the fishing species, an example being the Brown-hooded Kingfisher (*Halcyon albiventris*). Others, such as the small Striped Kingfishers (*Halcyon chelicuti*), nest in tree holes and even in holes in buildings, and sometimes occur in semi-deserts. The most well-known kingfisher, even though it may come as a surprise to find that it is one, is the Australian Kookaburra or Laughing Jackass (*Dacelo novaeguineae*), which eats venomous snakes and serves to control these reptiles in the Australian bush.

Abyssinian Ground Hornbills attacking a lizard

Larks sing to attract their mates and also have a peculiar fluttering and hovering courtship flight, and by similar visual and auditory displays most of the open space birds attract the attention of the opposite sex. In some species the display is mutual and the hens are as vigorous as the males. In the courtship dance of the African Crowned Cranes (*Balearica pavonina*) the cock bird bows to the hen with his neck bent and then jumps several feet into the air, trumpeting. The hen then joins in. Similarly the Sarus Cranes (*Grus antigone*) of the open, but well-watered plains of central India bow to each other and leap around with outstretched wings. Mutal displays can be made in flight by the aerial species, and the courtship flight of the buzzards (*Buteo* spp.) is most unusual. They fly one above the other in large circles, when the lower one turns completely over for a moment and they hook claws.

In the terrestrial species where sexual dimorphism is most apparent the specialized ornamentations of the males are brought into play, and this is particularly remarkable in several species of bustards (Otididae). The sexes live apart and only meet for mating purposes, the male attracting his potential mate with an impressive display. Some species have pectoral sacs which they incorporate into their display, and in the Australian Bustard (*Ardeotis australis*) it is covered with feathers and reaches the ground when extended. The large Kori Bustard (*Ardeotis kori*) has been described as almost turning itself inside out when displaying. A small species from India, the Lesser Florican (*Sypheotides indica*) jumps above the tall grass and floats down with outstretched tail, calling all the time, a display obviously evolved to overcome the difficulty of locating a mate in the tall grassland in which they live.

The male Jackson's Whydah or Widow-bird (*Drepanoplectes jacksoni*) makes a circular display arena by clearing away all debris around a central tuft of grass, which is left untouched. He dances around this tuft, jumping into the air with his tail feathers spread. When a female approaches he displays to her on the ground and after mating has taken place the hen goes off to raise her family alone. The related bishop-

The courtship display of Jackson's Whydah

bird males build several nests and conduct a female to each, and afterwards spend most of their time patrolling their territory busily keeping things in order.

In the grasslands most birds nest during the wet season, or at least towards the end of it, when there is a more plentiful supply of food available. In parts of Africa it is possible that the regular burning of the grasslands during the dry season may have had some effect on the birds' breeding habits.

The terrestrial species usually lay their eggs directly on to the soil in a small scrape or depression, but the eggs are so well camouflaged in shades of brown, with blotches, streaks or spots that they are difficult to find. In most cases the young are covered with down and are able to leave the nest soon after they hatch. They are said to be nidifugous, as opposed to the helpless nidicolous young of most tree-nesting birds which are naked and immobile when they hatch. Nidifugous chicks seldom leave their parents' sides, although some species such as the sandgrouse leave their chicks when they fly off for water. Solitary nesting is the rule for the

Tufted Guineafowl at nest

Carmine Bee-eaters

ground-nesters, whereas many of the arboreal grassland birds nest in large colonies, of which several species of weavers and bee-eaters are typical. There is of course 'safety in numbers' for these birds which produce helpless young and which would suffer severely from predators if their chicks were not protected in the early stages of their life. Inaccessible sites are chosen, the bee-eaters tunnelling into steep sandbanks where they are safe from most predators. The ground-nesting larks are exceptions as their nidicolous nestlings are helpless and vulnerable in the nest, which is often little more than a scrape of the soil behind some rocks.

The African grasslands are the home of the viduine whydahs which are host specific brood parasites. The hen whydah lays up to three eggs in the nest of a particular species of waxbill; the Fischer's Whydah (*Vidua fischeri*), for instance, lays her eggs in the nest of the Purple Grenadier (*Estrilda ianthinogaster*). It is essential that they lay in the correct nests as the waxbills will only feed young that show the same begging behaviour and down-patterning as their own nestlings. Unlike the Cuckoo (*Cuculus canorus*), these tropical parasites do not eject the rightful nestlings.

The down-covered mobile chicks of the terrestrial grassland birds would be easy prey for the many snakes, large lizards, birds of prey and other predators that abound in the open spaces, if it were not for their protective colouring (mentioned previously) and their ability to freeze when danger threatens. Cries of alarm from the parent birds cause the well-camouflaged chicks to crouch down if the danger is close at hand, or they may be called away if there is less risk in doing this. Many grassland species, however, have a more ingenious method of distracting predators away from their young, and the most well-known form of distraction display is injury feigning. This is a ritualized form of behaviour that simulates injury in order to draw a predator away from the nest by making it appear that the injured parent bird would be easier game. Distraction display is brought about by conflicting motivations, when the adult bird's desire to respond to its flight reflexes to remove itself to a safe distance conflicts with the parental desire to protect its brood. The bird runs

in front of the predator calling plaintively, and apparently dragging a broken wing, and entices the intruder to follow it. Not surprisingly females tend to distract more convincingly than males.

Even Ostriches perform injury feigning while their chicks are very young, but at the age of four weeks this is hardly necessary as they can reach a top speed of 56 kilometres (35 miles) per hour, and are safe from most predators. Young birds that leave the nest immediately or soon after hatching have an inborn tendency to follow their parents, and in practically all instances are raised on insects and small invertebrates irrespective of their adult diet.

It has on many occasions been written that birds bring water to their nestlings, and it has been said that the male sandgrouse, a bird related to the pigeons yet resembling a grouse, soaks his breast feathers to carry water to his chicks. This has not been authenticated but there is proof that the young are given food and water by regurgitation. The adults' crops can hold about 29 grams (just over 1 ounce) of water when fully distended, and can be filled in just a few seconds, often long distances from where the chicks have been left.

The communal distraction display of Pratincoles

BIRDS OF THE RIVERS, LAKES AND MARSHES

There are innumerable species of birds in the tropics that habitually enter the water to obtain their food, and others that live in close association with water. They are found in a wide variety of habitats, from open water to the swamps and marshes that are collectively known as the 'wetlands'. There are many large lakes in Africa, particularly in the east, and there are others in Central America (Lake Nicaragua), in Cambodia (Tonle Sap) and many other countries. In addition to these natural lakes several man-made lakes have been created in recent years, the largest examples being Afobaka in Surinam and Kariba in Rhodesia.

The many large rivers in the tropics, such as the Amazon, Congo, Niger and Orinoco, are very wide for many miles from their mouths, and provide stretches of open water which rival some of the lakes. Where many of these rivers enter the sea there is a large delta and often extensive swamps, but there are also many inland swamps in the equatorial regions. The Sudd, a vast papyrus swamp on the upper reaches of the River Nile, is typical of these and there is much swampland around Lake Chad in West Africa. There are temporary marshes, too, such as the inundation areas that are flooded during the rainy season.

On the upper reaches of the rivers there is a marked difference in the bird life, depending upon the terrain and vegetation, and the narrower waterways are the home of several species of birds that are adapted to living near water, but do not enter it. They usually nest close to water, also, and along the heavily forested creeks of Guyana the Crimson Topaz Hummingbird (*Topaza pella*), a beautiful streamer-tailed species, builds its untidy nest on slender branches over-hanging the water. Several species of tyrant flycatchers (Tyrannidae) live near streams and in the marshes of northern South America also, and some species take insects off the water surface in flight.

Like the forested rivers of South America the hilly streams

(*Top to bottom*) Shining Blue Kingfisher, Goliath Heron, Darter, Chestnut-naped Forktail

of South East Asia also have a characteristic bird life, and two groups of passerines are familiar residents. They are the redstarts (*Phoenicurus* spp.) and the forktails (*Enicurus* spp.), both related to the thrushes (Turdinae), and they feed in the manner of the wagtails (Motacillidae), searching for insects amongst the boulders and spray-soaked rocks. Downstream in the more open waters, in the tidal estuaries and along the coasts, the White-bellied Sea Eagle (*Haliaetus leucogaster*) feeds upon fish and sea snakes that it scoops out of the water with its talons, and flocks of pelicans (Pelecanidae) fish in parties, swimming in a line or half circle, with their bills in the water, driving fish into the shallows. Many pelicans, apparently, are not fond of rough water and prefer to fish in lagoons. In East Africa they are seldom seen in the estuaries or the unsheltered waters of the great lakes.

Swamps are of two types, and the island of Trinidad provides good examples of both. The Nariva swamp is a characteristic freshwater Neotropical swamp, and is frequented by birds that are completely dependent upon water, such as the kingfishers and migrant ducks. But there are other birds, for example the Orange-winged Amazon Parrot (*Amazona amazonica*), the Red-bellied Macaw (*Ara manilata*) and the Blue and Yellow Macaw (*Ara ararauna*), which nest in the rotting tops of dying moriche palms that rise high above the swamp. These birds are not completely dependent upon swamps or their trees, of course, and would find alternative habitat in the forests if the moriche palms were not available. On the opposite side of the island is a completely different swamp of tidal, brackish water which has been colonized by the mangrove. The shallow water at low tide barely covers the thick mud and entanglement of stilt-like roots of the mangroves, and this swamp, typical of many others like it in Africa, Malaya and tropical coasts elsewhere, is the home of herons, egrets and ibises.

The mudbanks and sandbanks of the rivers, estuaries and lakes form another major 'water' habitat. They are the domain of the waders, which often rest in the shallow water in a characteristic one-legged stance.

African Fish Eagle (*top*) and Black Heron

The Neotropical region is well supplied with rivers and wetlands, and transportation by water is in many areas the quickest, and sometimes the sole, means of travel. The Guianas, a large area north of the Amazon watershed, is particularly well endowed with waterways, and its native name translates into 'land of water'. Surprisingly, however, these forested rivers are not over-stocked with birds, despite the fact that tropical America houses the richest bird fauna in the world. A traveller can spend several days on these waterways and yet see only an occasional heron, duck or kingfisher. Nearer the coast the bird life is more plentiful, and in many areas there still exist colonies of the peculiar Hoatzins (*Opisthocomus hoazin*). Peculiar because they are probably in some ways the most primitive of birds, and have a wing structure resembling that of the fossil *Archaeopteryx*. It is usually considered to be the 'missing link' between modern day birds and their reptilian ancestors. Long claws on the bend of the wing help the young birds to clamber about in the branches around the nest, and if they fall into the water they can swim well, above and below the surface. Hoatzins are mainly crepuscular, sedentary birds, which rest among the river-bank foliage during the hot hours, and feed at night on the leaves, flowers and fruit of certain marsh plants.

Along the sandy banks of the more open rivers and in the flooded savannahs, large Jabiru Storks (*Jabiru mycteria*) and Snowy Egrets (*Egretta thula*) search for frogs, fish and small mammals, and in this type of habitat can also be found the three species of screamers (Anhimidae), which are restricted to the South American tropical and subtropical regions. They look rather like large, long-legged geese, but unlike them have only partially webbed toes. Along the banks of heavily forested streams, the Sun Bittern (*Europyga helias*) can be found, and the forest floor adjoining the river bank is the home of the trumpeters (Psophiidae). An interesting bird of the southernmost tropical rivers is the parasitic Black-headed Duck (*Heteronetta atricapilla*), which is the only species that habitually lays its eggs in other ducks' nests.

Amazon Kingfisher and White-winged Trumpeter ;
Snowy Egret (*bottom left*) and American Jacana

Africa is the home of many species of waders during the non-breeding season, many of them visitors from the northern temperate regions. In East Africa twenty members of the Scolopacidae family occur, and all of them are winter visitors. The Redshank (*Tringa totanus*), Greenshank (*T. nebularia*) and Common Sandpiper (*T. hypoleucos*) belong to this family and are always found near water and often in large flocks. The Charadriidae family is largely tropical, however, and in Africa is represented by numerous species that inhabit the beaches of the lakes and banks of rivers. The Spur-winged Plover (*Hoplopterus spinosus*) and the White-headed Plover (*Vanellus albiceps*) are typical resident species which have a wide distribution across the centre of the continent.

Of the many unusual waterbirds in Africa the Shoebill (*Balaeniceps rex*), Saddle-billed Stork (*Ephippiorhynchus senegalensis*), Skimmer (*Rynchops flavirostris*), Palm Nut Vulture (*Gypohierax angolensis*) and the Goliath Heron (*Ardea goliath*) are probably unique. The Shoebill, at times included with the herons, at others with the storks, stands just over a metre ($3\frac{1}{2}$ feet) high and has slaty plumage and long black legs. Its most unusual feature, however, is its large bulging bill which

Some typical African waterbirds

White-fronted Sand Plover

Painted Snipe

is almost as broad as it is long. It hides during the day in the extensive papyrus swamps of the Sudan and hunts at night, but it is now a very rare bird.

The Saddle-billed Stork is the most handsome member of its family and has a heavy red bill with a black band around the middle, and a yellow shield at the base of the upper mandible. Like the Shoebill it is a bird of the swamps.

The African Skimmer or Scissor-bill has a vertically flattened, elongated lower bill and obtains its food by skimming over the surface with its lower bill just beneath the water.

Formerly called the Vulturine Fish Eagle, the Palm Nut Vulture feeds on dead fish, crabs and crayfish, yet it also eats the kernels of the oil palm.

More solitary than most herons the large Goliath Heron cannot be confused with the others because of its tall size and slow methodical flight. All of the rapier-billed waterbirds are capable of inflicting serious injury if they get within striking distance of a man's face, but the long, powerful bill of the Goliath Heron is practically lethal.

The shallow grassland marshes that are created during the

Pied Kingfisher

Lesser Moorhen

Indian waterbirds: Little Black Cormorant (*left*) and Ruddy Kingfisher

wet season in many areas have already been mentioned, and there is a particularly impressive example near the Taj Mahal in India. It is a natural depression covering a very large area which fills with water during the rains and provides an ideal home for the thousands of migrating waterfowl that come south from central and northern Asia. Fortunately the whole area, which was originally a hunting preserve of the former rulers of Bharatpur, is now a sanctuary and the birds are protected. Keoladeo Ghana, as it is known, is not just a haven for the migrants, however, and a large number of the country's resident birds can be seen there also. In one part of the lake almost 3,000 Painted Storks (*Ibis leucocephalus*) nest and it has been estimated that five tons of fish, frogs and other aquatic animals are consumed daily by these birds alone. During the period when the nestlings are being reared at least 100 tons of food must be eaten. They are rather comical-looking birds, and have long yellow bills that are slightly decurved at the tip. They are one of the commonest species and have a wide distribution in southern Asia.

Storks are larger than herons and have thicker bills, and one of the most peculiar Indian species is the Open-billed Stork (*Anastomus oscitans*), a common bird of the marshes. When its beak is closed there is a wide gap in the middle, which is thought to be an adaptation for feeding on large water snails. Spoonbills (*Platalea leucorodia*), White Ibises (*Threskiornis melanocephala*), White-breasted Waterhens (*Amaurornis phoenicurus*), kingfishers and several species of ducks are very plentiful too, but all these birds are out-numbered by the cormorants (Phalacrocoracidae). Resident White-necked Storks (*Dissowa episcopus*) and Sarus Cranes stalk through the shallow water searching for small animal life, and even a few of the rare Asiatic or Siberian White Cranes (*Grus leucogeranus*) visit the sanctuary from the north.

The Whiskered Tern (*Chlidonias hybrida*) is also a bird of the marshes, where it plunges into the water after fish, or stalks crabs, frogs and insects. The Indian Pond Heron or Paddy-bird (*Ardeola grayii*), which resembles an egret, has different feeding methods and prefers to stand at the water's edge waiting for its prey.

Much of the Australasian region occurs outside the tropics, but the whole of New Guinea and the northernmost parts of

Bar-headed Goose

Ruddy Crake

Australia are decidedly tropical. In New Guinea there are two major rivers – the Sepik and the Fly – along which are extensive swamps and lagoons, particularly near the mouth of the Fly. Along the northern coast of Australia there is also a great deal of swampland, which is often tidal, and many rivers drain into the Gulf of Carpentaria and the Timor Sea. The Pied or Magpie Goose (*Anseranas semipalmata*), a large black and white bird with long legs and a long neck, is one of the most characteristic birds of the area, and lives in large flocks in the swamps. It is unusual as it has only partially webbed front toes, whereas other ducks have complete webbing. The small Pink-eared Duck (*Malacorhynchus membranaceus*) is also unique as it has a peculiar soft flap at the tip of its bill – a special adaptation for feeding on algae. The world's smallest waterfowl are represented in both countries by the Green Pygmy Goose (*Nettapus pulchellus*) of southern New Guinea, and the Australian Pygmy Goose (*Nettapus coromandelianus albipennis*) of north-eastern Australia.

The swamps of New Guinea are the home of several species

Australasian waterbirds:
Chestnut Rail (*left*) and Nankeen Night Heron;

of birds that appear to be restricted in their distribution to trees growing in or alongside water, and to reed beds. The Broad-billed Flycatcher (*Myiagra ruficollis*) is restricted to the mangrove swamps, and there are many warblers in the freshwater swamps. The Swamp Gerygone Warbler (*Gerygone magnirostris*) is a small insectivorous bird which lives in trees growing in water and along river banks and builds its nest on branches overhanging water. The Fly River Grass Warbler (*Megalurus albolimbatus*) is said to be a common species of the reed beds, floating rice grass and lotus lilies of the middle Fly River, and has been found nowhere else; and on the same lagoons occurs the Great Reed Warbler (*Acrocephalus arundinaceus*), which lives in the tall reed beds.

The feeding behaviour of the waterbirds has evolved into two basic forms. There are the long-legged wading birds which seek their food in the shallows or on the mudbanks, by striking, sifting or probing; and there are the swimmers which may dive for food or obtain it on or just below the surface. Their food may be vegetable, animal or a combination of both. One group of the long-legged species is actually

Pied or Magpie Goose (*left*) and Black Swan

referred to as 'the waders', and in general they have short, straight bills for probing into the mud. An exception is the Avocet (*Recurvirostra avosetta*), which has a long, recurved bill for feeding from the water surface.

Long rapier-like bills belong to the herons, egrets and storks, whose characteristic method of feeding is to stand motionless in shallow water, waiting for a fish or crab to come within striking distance of their bills, but they seldom spear their prey. Not all the herons have exceptionally long legs, however, and there are those which dash about in the swamps after their prey, or, as in the case of the Green Heron (*Butorides virescens*), dive off mangrove roots after fish. Other exceptions to the rule are the Boat-billed Heron (*Cochlearius cochlearius*) and the Shoebill, both of which scoop up fish and frogs with their boat-shaped beaks. Ibises (Threskiornithinae) have long, curved bills for probing into mud and under submerged stones; and the related spoonbills (Plataleinae) hold their long, flat spatulate bills almost horizontally and sweep them from side to side in the water, sifting out small crustaceans.

Most of these birds have long, slender legs and are able to walk into shallow water without getting their plumage wet, but they can swim when necessary, and some are able to dive. They have walking feet as opposed to swimming feet, however, although in several cases – such as the waders, for example – these may be webbed. The jacanas or lily-trotters (Jacanidae) have unusually long toes and claws which help to spread their weight when they are walking on floating vegetation. Leg length and specialized feeding habits reach their zenith in the flamingos (Phoenicopteridae), which turn their bills upside down to feed, and have filtering structures called lamellae within their bills to sift out small aquatic animals as the water flows through.

The legs and toes of the waterbirds are soft and leathery unlike the hard horny feet of the landbirds, and in the swimming species the feet have been virtually transformed into paddles. There are three types of swimming foot, the palmate, topipalmate and lobate. The latter type is characteristic of the coots (*Fulica* spp.) and grebes (Podicipitidae) and each toe has independent webs. Ducks (Anatidae) have the

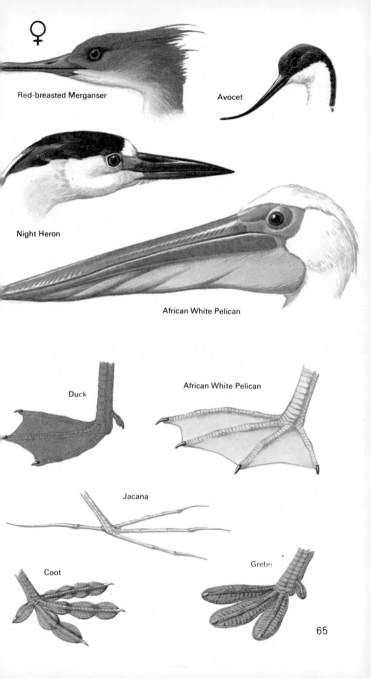

♀

Red-breasted Merganser

Avocet

Night Heron

African White Pelican

Duck

African White Pelican

Jacana

Coot

Grebe

65

palmate type of foot with a poorly developed hind toe that is free, and three forward-pointing toes linked with webs. The topipalmate variation of the waterbird foot occurs in the pelicans and cormorants and all four toes are webbed. Many swimming birds seek their food by diving, and some use their wings under water also, while those which rely solely on leg power have extra powerful thighs. The diving birds have less pneumatic skeletons than other birds, which means an increase in their specific gravity, bringing it nearer to that of the water. Consequently it takes less energy to remain submerged, and more effort can be put into finding food. Most have dense waterproofed plumage, but the cormorants and darters (Anhingidae) become sodden after swimming and need to perch with their wings extended to dry off. After an underwater chase in which the stiff tail is used as a rudder, darters often spear their prey and bring it to the surface, where it is tossed into the air, caught and swallowed. The best divers have their legs situated far back, and this is particularly noticeable in the aquatic, deep-diving Tufted Ducks (*Aythya fuligula*). Coots are also mainly aquatic and bring plants to the surface to eat, but the long-toed gallinules (*Porphyrio* spp.) rarely dive even though they do have narrow strips of skin along their toes to aid swimming.

Conversely, there are diving birds that do not swim. The fishing kingfishers, for example, take their prey by plunging into the water from a perch or after hovering, but they seldom stay long in the water. The Osprey (*Pandion haliaetus*) also submerges after fish but quickly takes to the air again. At the other extreme there are the dippers (Cinclidae) which can swim under water and can even walk on the bottom. They have dense plumage and a special membrane to protect their eyes when they are submerged.

In common with the grasslands and forests there are both solitary and colonial nesting waterbirds, and all manner of nest sites are used from trees, river banks and reed beds to water-lily leaves and even ledges underneath waterfalls. The jacanas are the 'floating nesters' and build their small pad of vegetation on to large leaves, and the weight of the bird often results in the eggs being partially submerged while they are being incubated. Other reports, however, suggest that the

Roseate Spoonbills

African Jacana (*Actophilornis africanus*) scoops its eggs up as it sits down to incubate and holds them against its sides with both wings.

The fishing kingfishers are the tunnelling experts and all species burrow into river banks for about a metre (several

feet). Tunnels of the Pied Kingfisher (*Ceryle rudis*) have measured 1·5 metres (5 feet) from the entrance to the nesting chamber, where the white eggs are laid directly on to the soil. Nest sanitation is practically unknown and the nestlings share the nest with accumulated droppings and fish bones. Other waterbirds – the pygmy geese, for instance – lay in holes high up in trees yet the unlikely-named Fulvous Tree Duck (*Dendrocygna bicolor*) nests in reed beds and long grass.

Solitary tree-nesters include fish eagles (*Haliaetus* spp.) which build large nests of sticks sometimes in use for many years, and the Hammerhead (*Scopus umbretta*) which builds a remarkable nest. This relative of the storks is only a small bird, yet it builds a structure of sticks lined with mud to form an enclosed chamber over a metre (3 to 4 feet) in diameter apart from the small side entrance tunnel. The much larger Whale-headed Stork or Shoebill nests on the ground, after flattening down a small area of grass on high ground.

Dippers build their domed nests in crevices in steep river banks, frequently close to waterfalls – and sometimes even underneath them – where their nests are continually moist on the outside.

All the species of flamingos (Phoenicopteridae) breed in large colonies, and in East Africa concentrations of almost one million pairs are not unknown. Their nests are simple cones of mud which the birds scoop up with their bills, and the one

Malachite Kingfisher sitting in nest burrow

or two eggs are laid in a shallow depression in the top. In East Africa the saline lakes are favoured as nesting grounds, particularly the centre of Lake Natron in Kenya, where many Lesser Flamingos (*Phoeniconaias minor*) nest. In 1962, however, they could not use Lake Natron as flooding made it unsuitable, and they were forced to nest on nearby Lake Magadi, where the nesting and hatching proved very successful. However, this lake has an exceptionally high mineral salt content, and a brittle crust of soda forms over the surface of the shallow water. When the nestlings left their soda nests they broke through this crust and the adhering particles hardened around their legs in the temperature of 140°F and quickly built up to drag the unfortunate nestlings into the soda water where they perished. It was estimated that out of the 800,000 young birds hatched almost half died, but many thousands more would have perished had not a rescue operation been launched by volunteers working in atrocious conditions.

Scarlet Ibises flying in to rookery

Fortunately, not all waterbirds are subjected to these natural disasters although there are instances of the nesting colonies of pelicans being flooded resulting in the destruction of nests and eggs. Like the jacanas others build floating nests of vegetation, an example being the Indian Whiskered Tern (*Chlidonias hybrida*), but most of the highly colonial terns nest on sandbanks where they lay their eggs directly on to the ground.

All the herons and many of the ibises are gregarious in the nesting season. In Africa the Cattle Egret (*Bubulcus ibis*) nests in association with the Sacred Ibis (*Threskiornis aethiopica*), whereas in the mangroves of South America it nests alongside Scarlet Ibis (*Eudocimus albus*), Boat-billed Herons (*Cochlearius cochlearius*), Little Blue Herons (*Hydranassa caerulea*) and night herons (*Nycticorax* spp.) about a metre (a few feet) above the water. True to its name, the night heron sets off to feed as the egrets and ibises are coming in to roost, and the Boat-billed Heron or Boatbill is a nocturnal bird also.

Parental care varies a great deal from species to species. Some male birds have nothing at all to do with the young birds; in other species the males may not take part in incubating or brooding yet bring food to the nestlings. The extreme form of behaviour occurs in the nesting habits of the Pheasant-tailed Jacana (*Hydrophasianus chirurgus*), which is polyandrous, the females leaving the whole business of incubation and chick rearing to the males. A hen may lay as many as eight clutches of eggs in a season, with four eggs in each clutch, and she must associate with more than one male as one pair can hardly undertake to rear more than two broods annually. This peculiar state of affairs also occurs in other wetland birds, for example the Bronze-winged Jacana (*Metopidius indicus*) and the painted snipe (Rostratulidae); it is thought to have evolved in order to relieve the hen of the task of incubating the eggs and rearing the young so that she could devote more time to greater egg production, to offset the high infantile loss. The success of this arrangement

Greater Flamingos watching over 'crèche'

obviously depends upon a preponderance of males.

There seems to be no record of polyandry in the African Jacana or Lily-trotter (*Actophilornis africana*), and both parents have been observed caring for the nestlings, although this is hardly a suitable name for the chicks which leave the nest soon after hatching and follow the adults over the lily leaves. They are able to dive and swim under water to escape danger, but an adult bird has been filmed carrying her chicks beneath her wings, held firmly to her sides with their spidery legs dangling.

Many species of birds do not tolerate the young of an earlier brood when a later nesting cycle is underway, but moorhens (*Gallinula* spp.) which nest in India during the south-west monsoons, not only tolerate them but allow them to feed their latest young. Peculiar parental behaviour has also been observed in the Greater Flamingo (*Phoenicopterus ruber roseus*), where the young of a number of pairs are pooled in a crèche, and are 'cared for' by a few adult birds.

African Jacana carrying young under its wing

THE BIRDS OF THE TROPICAL MOUNTAINS

The tropical mountains show a great diversity of bird life, ranging from the many species inhabiting the luxuriant jungles on the lower slopes to the sparse populations of the high alpine regions. Below 1,000 metres (3,000 feet) is considered to be lowland forest, but the altitudinal zones are seldom clear-cut boundaries that form barriers to the avifauna, but blend into each other with recessions on either side. On the slopes of the highest mountains there has been telescoped a complete range of vegetation from the sparse lichens of the polar regions to the luxuriant jungles of the tropics, all within the space of perhaps 16 kilometres (10 miles). In each zone there is a marked difference in rainfall, temperature and vegetation, which has resulted in the great mountain ranges of the tropics harbouring a greater abundance and variety of birds than any other region in the world.

Apart from the seasonal migration of some species the avi-

Vegetation and climatic zones of the Andes

Ice desert and sub-Antarctic steppe	5,000 m
Parámo Zone	3,000 m
Temperate Zone	2,400 m
Subtropical Zone	1,500 m
Tropical Zone	

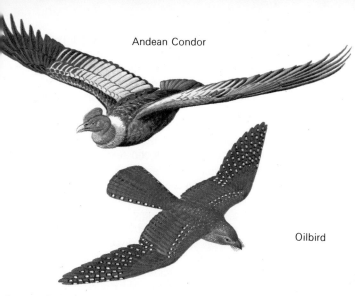

Andean Condor

Oilbird

fauna of the mountain slopes is adapted to the conditions prevailing in its chosen habitat, and does not wander into the adjoining zonal habitats. Characteristic species of the subtropical zone at 1,500 to 2,400 metres (5,000 to 8,000 feet) are unlikely to occur in the temperate zone at an altitude of 3,000 metres (10,000 feet) and vice versa. In addition, the temperature and vegetation – or lack of it – of extensive mountain ranges form a barrier which prevents the movement of species from one side of the range to the other. Likewise, where there are adjoining ranges the dividing lowlands also form an effective barrier for the temperate zone and higher altitude species. The result is that subspecies evolve, and the species is said to be polytypic. This is particularly noticeable in Colombia, where the Andes branch into three arms. For example, the Ornate Flycatcher (*Myiotriccus ornatus*) of the western slope of the Andes is represented by one subspecies on the eastern slope of the eastern Andes, and another on the western slope of the western Andes.

In some regions there may even be variation in the zones between the seasons, and in the Andes of Colombia for instance, the snow-line, normally at 4,650 metres (15,500 feet), may vary a hundred or so metres (several hundred feet) depending upon the annual rainfall and the temperature.

Practically all the tropical mountains are forest-clad right up to the snow-line, and they are the home of many representatives of bird families that appear in the lowland forests. The Quetzal (*Pharomachrus mocinno*) for instance, of the mist-laden Central American cloud forests above 3,000 metres (10,000 feet), is a member of the trogon family (Trogonidae) which is well represented in the humid lowland forests. Similarly, above 2,400 metres (8,000 feet) in the Andes the mountain tanagers replace the tanager species that occur on the lower elevations and in the flood plains, although there is some intermingling in the subtropical zone. The foothills and middle slopes are usually the home of a greater variety of birds as they offer a wider range of habitats and conditions, but birds can exist on the higher slopes wherever food is available. For example, Gay's Seedsnipe (*Attagis gayi*) lives in the páramo zone of the Andes up to 5,000 metres (17,000 feet), where freezing winds, snow and ice combine to produce a barren wilderness in which it is surprising that any form of life can be sustained.

Motmots (Momotidae) are birds of the tropical zone forests up to 1,500 metres (5,000 feet), but in Central America the Blue-throated Motmot (*Aspatha gularis*) lives in the oak and pine forests up to 3,000 metres (10,000 feet), where heavy frosts are experienced in winter. Where a species occurs in both low and high altitude habitats altitudinal variation may exist, in that there is a diminution in size from the high altitude regions to the lowlands. As Sir Julian Huxley has said, the body size of a subspecies usually increases with the decreasing mean temperature of its habitat. In brief, the warmer the climate the smaller the subspecies, which holds good for almost ninety per cent of the birds investigated. This is particularly noticeable between birds of the same species from the Himalayas and Malaya.

Another interesting fact is that the maximum depth of pigmentation occurs in hot and humid climes, and this decreases as the temperature decreases up the mountain slopes, within the same species of course.

Quetzal at nest hole; Blue-crowned Chlorophonia (*inset*)

PERU

Lake Titicaca

Laguna de Salinas

BOLIVIA

Arica

Lake Poopo

Lake Coipas

CHILE

PACIFIC
OCEAN

Laguna Colorada

Lake Verde

Mud flats and dried up lakes

Lakes

High in the Andes there are a number of remote lakes that are the home of some interesting waterbirds about which comparatively little is known. In fact one species of flamingo was only recently rediscovered there, after a lapse of almost a century. In 1866 an expedition sponsored by Berkely James, a British businessman, discovered a new species of flamingo in the high salt lakes of Chile at an elevation of about 4,200 metres (14,000 feet), which was named the James Flamingo (*Phoenicoparrus jamesi*) after him. Until then it was believed that only the rare Andean Flamingo (*P. andinus*), and the common Chilean (*Phoenicopterus chilensis*) and Roseate (*P. roseus*) Flamingos occurred in South America. The remoteness of the area defied all further attempts to locate the new species, and the museum specimens had faded so much that the authenticity of the James Flamingo was beginning to be doubted. In 1956, however, it was rediscovered in the mountain lakes of Peru and Bolivia by a group of Chileans and an American, and in the same year they

High altitude lakes in the Andes

discovered thousands of these birds nesting on Laguna Colorada in Bolivia.

These high altitude lakes are also the home of several species of coots and grebes, and two species of the latter – the Short-winged Grebe (*Centropelma micropterum*) and the Junin Grebe (*Podiceps taczanowskii*) – are flightless. The Short-winged Grebe lives on Lake Titicaca, 3,700 metres (12,500 feet) above sea level on the Peru/Bolivia border, and the other species is found only on Lake Junin in Peru. The Colombian Eared Grebe (*Podiceps andinus*) occurs on Lake Tota in Colombia at a height of about 2,700 metres (9,000 feet).

The Giant Coot (*Fulica gigantea*) and the Horned Coot (*Fulica cornuta*) breed in the small mountain lakes of the Andes, usually above 3,900 metres (13,000 feet) in the zerophytic zone, and the Horned Coot has the unusual habit of building a nest of stones in the absence of other nesting material.

In the swamps of the páramo zone live the resident Andean Snipe (*Gallinago andina*) and the winter visiting Common Snipe (*Gallinago gallinago*), and in the more open waters the Andean Teal occurs. In the mountains torrents of all zones up

James Flamingo

Andean Flamingo

Sword-billed Hummingbird in high Andes

to the páramo live the Torrent Ducks (*Merganetta armata*), slimly built diving ducks with long, stiff tails. But the most surprising birds to see in these regions are surely humming-birds.

When the famous bird collector, Charles Cordier, was collecting rare mountain birds for the New York Zoo in Ecuador in 1949, he secured Chimborazo Hillstar Humming-birds (*Oreotrochilus chimborazo*) at an altitude of 4,200 metres (14,000 feet) where bare rocks, frost, rain and fog are common-place, but these small birds are well adapted for life in such a habitat. Some live even higher up the slopes, and the Bearded Helmet-crest (*Oxypogon guerinii*) can be seen on the bushy parts of the páramo zone at 4,800 metres (16,000 feet) above sea level. Hummingbirds are among the most highly special-ized of all birds, and their incessant activity is powered by the intake of several times their own weight of energy-rich food daily. They must feed every few minutes upon flower nectar and small insects to provide the food they require, and are, of course, most plentiful in the subtropical zone of the Andes, where the warm, moist climate and dense vegetation provide a suitable habitat for a large population.

Irrespective of the air temperature, when hummingbirds roost their body temperature is lowered and they become torpid. This results in a considerable saving of energy as there is less heat loss than occurs in other birds. They are in fact the only birds that undergo a daily cycle of torpidity. Many days in these inhospitable regions are fog-bound, so the hummingbirds cannot rely on the direct warmth of the sun's rays to revive them in the morning. However cool the day temperature may be, they revive early in the morning as the saving of energy resulting from torpidity, compared with the heat loss from a sleeping bird, leaves sufficient to allow the birds to 'warm up'.

Some species do migrate up and down the mountain slopes, an example being the Santa Marta Sabrewing (*Campylopterus phainopeplus*). It lives in the Santa Marta Mountains of Colombia up to 1,800 metres (6,000 feet) in the early part of the year, but ranges up to 4,500 metres (15,000 feet) from June to October.

Map showing high altitude regions of the tropics

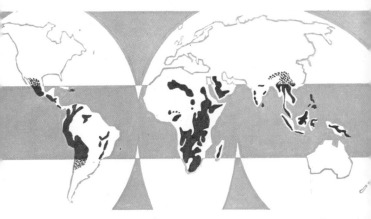

BIRDS OF THE TROPICAL ISLANDS

Borneo

Borneo is the third largest island in the world and is included in the Malaysian subregion of the Oriental zoogeographic region. The island's avifauna includes many Malaysian species but is more specialized; it has no relationship with that of the Indian and Indo-Chinese subregions.

Practically all of Borneo is forested, mainly primary with large areas of secondary forest. The lowland birds occur in the floodplains and the foothills, and many of these species also occur in Malaysia and Sumatra. This is because the Sunda Shelf – the shallow sea between the islands of Borneo, Sumatra and Java, and the Malay peninsula – was until 20,000 years B.C. much shallower than its present depth of 90 metres (300 feet), and parts of the shelf were exposed. A land bridge therefore existed over which animals from the South East Asian mainland migrated.

There is a sharp division in the island's avifauna at about 900 metres (3,000 feet) above which the montane species occur, and the majority of the birds endemic to Borneo live in the montane forest and scrub. In these forests from 1,200 metres (4,000 feet) upwards, the tropical vegetation is

Bulwer's Pheasant

Blue-headed Pitta

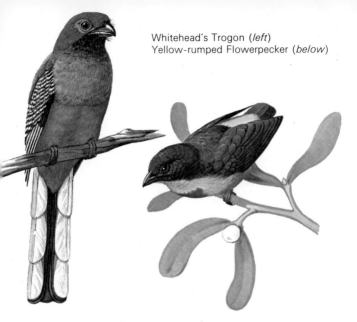

Whitehead's Trogon (*left*)
Yellow-rumped Flowerpecker (*below*)

replaced by oaks and other temperate climate trees, even conifers. This is in contrast to the altitudinal zones of the larger landmasses where the temperate zone commences at about 2,450 metres (8,000 feet). The attractive Bulwer's Pheasant (*Lophura bulweri*) is a submontane species that is endemic to Borneo, whereas the Argus Pheasant (*Argusianus argus*) lives in the swampy lowlands and also occurs in Malaysia and Sumatra. With one exception all the montane species occur on Mount Kinabalu 4,101 metres (13,455 feet), the island's highest peak. The exception is the Black Oriole (*Oriolus hosii*), a black bird with chestnut undertail coverts. Whitehead's Trogon (*Harpactes whiteheadi*) is also confined to the island and ranges along the spinal chain from Mount Kinabalu to Mount Dulit.

Two of the most colourful of Borneo's endemic birds do not live in the montane regions however, but are common residents of the lowland forests. They are the Blue-headed Pitta (*Pitta baudi*) of the rain forest and the small Yellow-rumped Flowerpecker (*Prionochilus xanthopygius*) which occurs in secondary forest and clearings.

Woodpecker Finch using cactus thorn as probe

Large Ground Finch

The Galapagos Islands

Unlike heavily forested Borneo the Galapagos Islands are dry and mainly barren rocky outcrops, 1,600 kilometres (1,000 miles) off the coast of Ecuador. The avifauna there has evolved in an isolated environment, far enough away from the mainland to prevent many landbirds reaching the archipelago. This freedom from competition has allowed a greater ecological divergence. The geographical isolation of subspecies has been possible on many islands, and when these have evolved along different ecological lines natural selection increases this divergence if the subspecies' range overlaps later on.

It was in the Galapagos that Charles Darwin first became convinced of the reality of evolution, and he was so inspired that he produced his classic *Origin of Species* some years later. This archipelago of volcanic origin is thought to have risen from the sea about three million years ago, and it is generally believed that it has never been connected to the mainland. Darwin was struck by the basic similarities of the finches that he brought back with him, their main differences being in the shape of their bills and their feeding habits; and he came to the conclusion that they had a common ancestor. There are thirteen species of these birds, now known as

Darwin's finches (Geospizinae), and they show remarkable adaptations to fit ecological niches, which were apparently unoccupied at the time by competitors. The Large Ground Finch (*Geospiza magnirostris*) has a heavy seed-crushing beak, whereas the Warbler Finch (*Certhidea olivacea*) has the bill of a typical insectivorous bird. The most highly adapted of all is the Woodpecker Finch (*Camarhynchus pallidus*), which lacks the woodpeckers' drilling beak and long tongue, but manages to probe insects from their holes in trees by using cactus spines and twigs – one of the few cases in which a bird uses a tool for feeding. The only group of birds comparable to the Darwin's finches are the honeycreepers (*Drepanididae*) of the Hawaiian islands, which also show a high degree of adaptive radiation.

Not only were competitors absent on the islands but, before the arrival of man and his introduced animals, predators also, and another Galapagos bird that has evolved in this idyllic setting is the Flightless Cormorant (*Nannopterum harrisi*). Its wings are useless for flying but are still held out to dry in the manner of the other cormorants (Phalacrocoracidae).

Male Golden Bowerbird at bower; this species is endemic to New Guinea.

New Guinea

New Guinea, the second largest island in the world and the largest tropical one, and some of its small neighbouring islands form the Papuan subregion of the Australasian region. Like the association of Borneo with the Asiatic mainland long ago, land bridges existed between New Guinea and Australia during the Tertiary period (from about seventy to two million years ago) and although the ancestors of the region's birds originated from the Oriental zoogeographic region, the island has been cut off from the Asian mainland since before modern birds evolved. Consequently many characteristic Oriental birds such as pheasants, barbets and woodpeckers, are absent; but there are a number of endemic species.

New birds of New Guinea have evolved in a tropical environment where the rainfall is high, and the difference between them and Australian birds is mainly an ecological one. The island is mostly covered with evergreen forest, rain forest in the lowlands, and temperate forests

The inverted display of the Blue Bird of Paradise

at higher elevations on mountains. There are also extensive grasslands in the lowlands and several large areas of mountain grassland. The large ground pigeons are peculiar to the sub-region, and are common birds of the lowland forests. The largest is Scheepmaker's Crowned Pigeon (*Goura scheepmakeri*) which reaches almost a metre (3 feet) in length. The crowned pigeons (*Goura* spp.) are reluctant to use their wings, and prefer to walk or run away from danger, and are obviously evolving into flightless birds in the relative absence of natural predators. The cassowaries (*Casuarius* spp.) have already lost the power of flight and have developed a high degree of specialization of their legs and a completely terrestrial way of life. The Double Wattled Cassowary (*Casuarius casuarius*) stands 1·8 metres (6 feet) high and has a blade-like casque, which is thought to have evolved as a protective shield for when the bird charges through the undergrowth with its head held low. The innermost of the three toes on each foot is armed with a long, sharp claw, and there are several records of humans being killed by a well-placed forward kick.

Magnificent Bird of Paradise displaying

The West Indies

Although included in the Neotropical region where the bird life is the richest on earth, the West Indies are poorly represented. They received their birds from Central and North America long ago, and the avifauna has often been referred to as 'tropical North American'. But there are also many characteristic birds, including some that are endemic to particular islands, and a species of hummingbird that is the world's smallest bird. The birds of Trinidad and Tobago have been derived from South America, and many of those occurring on the islands of Bonaire, Curaçao and Aruba also came from that continent, but even on these islands there is not the diversity of the mainland.

Birds peculiar to the West Indies include a number of hummingbirds. The Bee Hummingbird (*Mellisuga helenae*), a mere 6 centimetres (2½ inches) long, of which at least half consists of beak and tail, is found only on Cuba and the neighbouring Isle of Pines. It is little larger than a bumblebee and is often mistaken for one. Another small species is the Vervain Hummingbird (*Mellisuga minima*) which occurs only on the islands of Hispaniola and Jamaica. On the latter island lives the most impressive bird of the whole area, the Streamer-tailed Hummingbird or Long-tailed Doctor Bird (*Trochilus*

Bananaquit

Jamaican Tody

Streamer-tailed Hummingbird

polytmus) which has two elongated black tail feathers almost 15 centimetres (6 inches) long which hum when the bird is flying.

The todies (Todidae) belong to a family of birds confined to the Greater Antilles; and Cuba, Jamaica and Puerto Rico each has a representative, and Hispaniola two. With a maximum length of 11 centimetres (4½ inches) all the species have the same colour scheme of green upperparts and red throat, and vary in the pink, green and white shading of their underparts. Like their close relatives the motmots they dig their own nesting tunnels in earth banks, and lay their white eggs directly on to the soil in the nest chamber at the end of the tunnel 60 centimetres (2 feet) long.

Heavy forest still covers a number of the islands and this is an ideal habitat for the terrestrial quail doves, (*Geotrygon* spp.), which have the habits of the Old World pheasants, except that they nest in trees. Several endemic species occur on Cuba and Jamaica, where the forests also shelter parrots that are now quite rare. Jays (Corvidae) abound in Central America yet are absent in the West Indies, whereas crows (*Corvus* spp.) do not occur on the mainland yet are represented by no less than four species.

The Philippines

There are 7,100 islands in the Philippine group, and from the ornithologist's point of view they are probably the most interesting islands in the world. Interesting because there are so many small islands inhabited by birds that are restricted to small islands. Large islands do not seem to suit these birds, as breeding places at least, but they may visit them to feed. Strangely the best examples of these birds are all pigeons – the terrestrial Nicobar Pigeon (*Caloenas nicobarica*), the arboreal Nutmeg Imperial Pigeon (*Ducula bicolor*) and Grey Imperial Pigeon (*Ducula pickeringi*). The Philippines are also interesting because examples can be seen on the various islands of normally high-altitude birds living at lower altitudes on the small islands. On the large island of Luzon, for example, Merrill's Fruit Pigeon (*Ptilinopus merrilli*) occurs on the mountain slopes, yet on the nearby small island of Polillo it lives in the forests at sea level. Also, the small island birds may live in a different habitat to that occupied by the same species on the larger islands. The Metallic Wood Pigeon (*Columba vitiensis*) lives in the primaeval forests of the large island of Negros, but on smaller islands it has been found in brush and open forest. This may of course be due to the fact that many of the Philippine islands have been practically denuded of their original forest to grow crops, and these changes of habitat have occurred in fairly recent times. If this is the case it is indeed fortunate for the birds that they were able to adapt to the new habitat, as there are many examples of birds throughout the world that have perished when they lost their habitat to man.

The Philippines are not noted for pigeons only, however. The malcohas (Phaenicophaeinae) are colourful birds, but they are not parasitic and build their own nests and raise their own families. The most well-known bird is the huge Monkey-eating Eagle (*Pithecophaga jefferyi*), a powerful bird of prey that is rapidly diminishing in numbers owing to the destruction of its forest habitat and, in the past at least, to trapping for the zoo and curio trade.

(*Top to bottom*) Chestnut Manakin, Oriental White-eye, Black-naped Blue Monarch, Fairy Bluebird

Birds of the Indian Ocean Islands

Yellow-eared Bulbul

Emerald-collared
Parakeet

Ceylonese Grackle

Nicobar Pigeon

The Islands of the Indian Ocean

The avifauna of the islands and island groups of the tropics is closely related to that of the nearest mainland in most instances, and this is nowhere more noticeable than in the Indian Ocean.

The birds of the Nicobar Islands off the western coast of Sumatra are closely related to the birds of the Malay peninsula and archipelago – the Malaysian subregion of the Oriental zoogeographic region. Those of the Andaman Islands further north have closer affinities with Burma, which is included in the Indo-Chinese subregion. Ceylon belongs to the Indian subregion and its birds have close affinities with the birds of Europe and northern Asia. Strangely, several species common in India do not occur on Ceylon. The Black (*Coragyps atratus*) and Bengal or White-backed Vultures (*Gyps bengalensis*) for instance are completely absent, and the Egyptian Vulture (*Neophron percnopterus*) rarely occurs, even though all three species are powerful fliers and could quite easily cross from the mainland.

Malagasy (formerly Madagascar) has recently been accorded regional status – the Malagasy region – as its birds are sufficiently different from those of the Ethiopian region. The Comoro Islands, lying between Malagasy and the mainland, have a transitional avifauna. It is probable that most of the Malagasy birds are descendants of stock that originally came from Africa. Of its 185 species sixty-five per cent are endemic, but there has been such great specific differentiation that each genus averages just over one species each.

Most of the Malagasy forest has been cleared, but there is still a large area of evergreen woodland on the eastern side where the rainfall is high. Wooded and often eroded grassland covers much of the island now. Although there was originally a large forest area, there are relatively few frugivorous birds. One of these is the Velvety Asity (*Philepitta castanea*), which resembles the sunbirds (Nectariniidae) and feeds on small berries in the thick forest undergrowth. Two species of the peculiar vangas (Vangidae), the Hook-billed Vanga (*Vanga curvirostris*) and the Helmetbird (*Aerocharis prevostii*), are practically carnivorous and feed upon small amphibians and reptiles in addition to insects.

BIRDS OF THE TOWNS AND GARDENS

Throughout South and Central America, on the roofs of abattoirs, on refuse tips and anywhere else that offal or carrion is available there is quite likely to be a whole regiment of Black Vultures waiting to act as undertakers. One of the most repugnant sights in the New World tropics is a group of these birds dismembering a dog killed on the road. In India and Africa the common Egyptian Vulture is the main scavenger, but it is ably assisted by the Hooded Vulture (*Necrosyrtes monachus*) in Africa and the Bengal or White-backed Vulture in India. Whatever inhibitions we may have about these birds tearing at road casualty animals, or stalking around the environs of some tropical towns searching for human excrement and offal, they do serve a most useful function. When large food items have been sighted they assemble *en masse* and rapidly reduce a breeding ground for disease to a pile of cleanly picked bones.

Other favourite sites of these scavengers are the fish wharves and coastal fishing villages, where they eagerly await the offal from gutted fish, or the unsuitable fish species that are discarded. As the young vultures are reared on a diet of regurgitated carrion, they are well prepared for this type of food when adult. Scavenging is not restricted to the vultures, however. Two related species of storks, the African Marabou (*Leptoptilos crumeniferous*) and the Indian Adjutant (*Leptoptilos dubius*), both feed in association with the vultures. Association is hardly the correct word though, as these storks are large birds – over a metre (almost 4 feet) tall – and have powerful beaks, and the vultures are careful to stand well clear until the storks have finished. The House Crow (*Corvus splendens*) of India is also a beneficial scavenger and eats virtually anything from dead rats to offal. Also in India two very common kites, the Brahminy Kite (*Haliastur indus*) and the Common Black or Pariah Kite (*Milvus miarans*), regularly include offal in their otherwise normal raptorial diet. The former frequents seaports where it gathers scraps thrown overboard from vessels, and the Pariah Kite is a bird of the built-up areas, even the cities, where it swoops on scraps along the busiest thoroughfares.

Egyptian Vulture (*left*) and Marabou Stork

The range of the Brahminy Kite extends through South East Asia and into the Malay peninsula, where it is a common scavenger in the coastal areas and at ports. Much of Malaysia is still primaeval forest and it has often been said that the jungle is never far away from civilization, even from the largest cities. Also the width of the peninsula dictates that the coast is never far away either, so the bird life of Malaysian gardens is basically of forest birds, with some coastal species, except of course in the hill stations. The birdwatcher there is fortunate indeed, as in many areas he need not move from his garden but still be able to study as many as sixty-five species of birds, which is the number that the authority on the birds of the Malay peninsula, Mr A. G. Glenister, saw in or from his garden in Ipoh, Perak.

One of the most colourful of the garden visitors is the black and yellow Black-naped Oriole (*Oriolus chinensis*), a winter visitor from the north which Dr Gibson Hill has described as one of the twelve commonest species of the gardens on the outskirts of Singapore. Its characteristic loud whistle draws attention to the bird as well as its brilliant plumage. Glossy Tree Starlings (*Aplonis panayensis*) are also frequent visitors to gardens when trees are in fruit, and sunbirds are plentiful too, the Brown-throated species (*Anthreptes malacensis*) in the vicinity of coconut palms, and the Yellow-breasted Sunbird (*Leptocoma jugularis*) which searches amongst the bushes for insects and flower nectar. Some of the most brightly coloured birds are often quite inconspicuous when they enter dense foliage, and both the colourful Copper-smith Barbet (*Megalaima haemacephala*), which is common in northern gardens, and the Scarlet-backed Flowerpecker (*Dicaeum cruentatum*) can often be heard but not seen. The opposite is the case where the handsome black and white Magpie Robin (*Copsychus saularis*) is concerned; it is one of the finest singers of all tropical birds and is a welcome visitor to gardens.

Trinidad is included zoogeographically with the South American mainland, and has an avifauna typical of that

(*Top to bottom*) Gaudy Barbet, Glossy Starling, Black-naped Oriole and Yellow-backed Sunbird

continent and not the West Indies. One of the commonest birds throughout the territory is the Kiskadee (*Pitangus sulphuratus*), one of the largest of the tyrant-flycatchers. Aggressive, noisy and colourful, its call has been interpreted as *Qu'est–ce qu'il dit*, and it is the most characteristic bird call to be heard on the island. Unlike most members of their family, which is basically insectivorous, the Kiskadees are the 'starlings' of the Neotropical gardens and eat frogs, lizards, mice and even young birds, in addition to fruit. They are just as likely to be attracted to a bunch of ripe bananas on a bird table as the frugivorous tanagers. Their large, untidy, globular-shaped nests are placed in prominent positions in trees and buildings.

The small Bananaquits (*Coereba flaveola*) are equally abundant, and like the Kiskadees are found in all types of habitat provided food is available to them. They are more conservative in their choice of food however, and need the typical honeycreeper diet of nectar and small insects, plus ripe fruit. They are very fond of ripe bananas, but can be attracted to gardens devoid of flowering and fruiting plants

(*Left to right*) Kiskadee, Blue Tanager, Bare-eyed Thrush and Silver-beaked Tanager

by providing sugar water. Two species of tanagers, the Blue Tanager (*Thraupis episcopus*) and the Palm Tanager (*Thraupis palmarum*) are also common garden visitors, and gardens bordered with secondary forest or cocoa plantations can expect visits from the more attractive Silver-beaked Tanager (*Ramphocelus carbo*).

The Neotropical gardens also have their orioles although these are not related to the Malayan species. The Black-throated Oriole (*Icterus nigrogularis*) is a frequent visitor to gardens, even in the capital city of Port of Spain. All of these birds attack ripening fruit, and even paddy grain spread out on mats to dry in the country gardens and along the roadsides is not free from bird attack. Two of the worst offenders are the parasitic Glossy Cowbird (*Molothrus bonariensis*) and the Boat-tailed Grackle (*Cassidix mexicanus*). Common in gardens and adjoining the central savannahs are the brown and grey Mockingbird (*Mimus polyglottos*) and the small Ruddy Ground Dove (*Columbigallina talpacoti*). The Bare-eyed Thrush (*Turdus nudigenis*), an avid feeder on fallen papaya and guava fruit, shares with the Kiskadee the title of the largest regular garden visitor.

Like the birds of the Trinidad and Malaysian gardens, many of those seen in the gardens of East Africa are basically forest

Fiscal Shrike (*top*) and Speckled Mousebird

species, together with a few grassland birds. The nearness of extensive grasslands or forest areas to the towns is perhaps even more apparent there than anywhere else in the world, although many of these areas are now being cultivated. Many birds are welcomed to gardens because they catch flies, or cross pollinate flowers, or are good songsters; while others are not as welcome because of the damage they cause to plants. The 'sparrow' of the East African gardens – the Streaky Seedeater (*Poliospiza gularis*) — is said to be a nuisance in the highlands because it damages plants; but the mousebirds or colies (*Colius* spp.) are the most destructive. There are four species in East Africa, and they are frequent visitors to gardens where they destroy fruit and flowers. To make matters worse they are gregarious and always travel in small parties; they are even partial to small unripe fruit, although they are by no means strict vegetarians as they have been observed to kill and eat other birds' nestlings.

Another bird with somewhat distasteful habits is the common Fiscal Shrike (*Lanius collaris*), which inhabits all types of country and is frequently seen in towns and gardens. Like most of the hawking birds it favours high vantage points from which it can scan the area for insects and other prey, often using telegraph wires for this purpose. Its local name of 'hangman' is derived from its habit of impaling young birds and other food items on a thorn or sisal spike for later use, which is of course characteristic of many species of shrikes.

Flycatchers (Tyrannidae) are welcome visitors, and East Africa has an abundance of these birds. The Dusky (*Alseonax adustus*), Pale (*Bradornis pallidus*) and Grey-headed (*Terpsiphone viridis*) Paradise Flycatchers are often to be seen in gardens, where they soon accept the closeness of man and become quite tame. Sunbirds are also common throughout the area, and the Scarlet-chested Sunbird (*Chalcomitra senegalensis*) feeds on flying ants and other insects and visits flowers for their nectar. The Olive Sunbird (*Cyanomitra olivacea*) frequently nests in gardens and on occasions has even nested under the eaves of houses.

Village Weaver (*bottom*) and Olive-bellied Sunbird

BIRDS OF THE CULTIVATIONS

From a bird's point of view there are two basic types of cultivations in the tropics. There are the crops which themselves provide food for some species of birds, and for others a habitat in which they can find food of other kinds and possibly nesting sites. Secondly, there are the crops which do not produce fruit or seeds acceptable to birds, although in a few instances their flowers may attract nectar-feeders. Examples of the first type, those that produce food for birds, are the cereal crops of wheat, millet and rice, and the fruit crops of guava, pawpaw, and sometimes bananas, except in the large commercial plantations where these are harvested before they are ripe. These extensive plantations in Central America and on some of the West Indian islands are obviously examples of the second type of 'cultivated habitat'. In addition vast coffee plantations exist in eastern Brazil, rubber plantations in Malaysia, and throughout the tropics, and particularly in the West Indies, Indonesia and the Pacific islands there are very large areas of coconut palms.

Birds have occupied the cultivated areas to benefit either from the habitat available to them or the abundance of food. In some instances it is a temporary arrangement, for example when they visit the plantations purely to feed, but there is evidence that others have no difficulty in adapting to this 'change' of habitat, when it closely resembles their natural niche and provides an equal or greater supply of food. There is also evidence that some locally migratory species can alter their habits to take advantage of crops ripening at a certain time of year.

Although cultivated land is providing a new habitat for birds it is not necessarily additional habitat. What must be borne in mind, of course, is that in most cases natural habitat areas were used in the first place to produce crops, but there is also evidence that some bird populations increase as a result of the extra food supply provided by man. In many parts of Asia large areas of the forested hillsides have been cleared to establish the terraced paddy fields. The situation in Borneo is typical; jungle is felled annually to provide rice lands to meet the ever increasing needs of the people, and the

103

amount of forest habitat available to birds is being reduced at the same rate. On the other hand those who irrigate fields in the uplands to grow wet paddy are providing the only open wetlands in the interior of the island for the phalaropes (Phalaropodidae), Great Reed Warblers and other passage migrants and winter visitors. For the phalaropes at least this is perhaps not such a good thing, as they are said to settle in flocks in the rice fields and the Kelabit tribesmen, who know just when to expect them, shoot many with their blowpipes. When the forest is cleared for terracing the birds are naturally forced into the adjoining jungle, where there will already be a resident population anyway; but when small areas of marsh are drained and cultivated there can be no such recourse for the sedentary marsh-dwellers. The endangered Nightingale Warbler (*Acrocephalus luscinia rehsei*) of the island of Nauru in the Pacific Ocean is being placed in just such a predicament at present.

Several seed-eating species that are now more or less dependent upon cultivated cereals have already been mentioned, but there are many other species that skulk about in the cover provided by these crops, some seeking purely insect food, others also eating small amounts of the cultivated seeds. Francolins, crakes and bustards seek their food in the wheat and millet fields of East Africa, while the rice fields of South East Asia provide a favourable habitat for snipe, whose bills are adapted for probing into the mud for molluscs, worms and aquatic insects. The Pintail Snipe (*Capella stenura*) is apparently a very particular bird, and prefers to feed in the rice fields when the water is barely evident above the ground; it avoids both flooded and dried out fields. White-breasted Water Hens (*Amaurornis phoenicurus*) and egrets (Ardeidae) are also frequently seen in the fields, searching for insects. There are both insectivorous and fish-eating kingfishers, ducks and hawks, and for part of the year the winter visitors and migrants from the north. In fact the rice fields probably provide food for a wider variety of birds than any other form of cultivation, as seed-eaters, waders, fishers, raptors and insect hawkers are all catered for.

Red-breasted (*top*) and Yellow-headed Marshbirds on rice

In the rice fields of the New World there is a completely different avifauna, apart from the ubiquitous Cattle Egrets (*Bubulcus ibis*). The commonest birds in the fields and adjoining wet savannahs of northern South America are the Yellow-headed Marshbird (*Agelaius icterocephalus*) and the Military Starling or Red-breasted Marshbird (*Leistes militaris*). They are both gregarious species and the small flocks enliven the rice fields with their colour. Rice is a fairly recent crop in this area, but the indigenous birds have welcomed this extra supply of food.

In most instances the tropical cultivations which do not themselves provide birds with food are more permanent ones, and furnish niches that some species are able to occupy. The Crested Tree Swift (*Hemiprocne longipennis*) for example, is a lowland bird of South East Asia, where it frequents the more open forests and jungle clearings, catching small insects on the wing. Since the introduction of rubber as a major crop in Malaysia this species has colonized the plantations. Another example of introduced and now widely cultivated plants providing a suitable habitat for native birds is the case of the Coucal or Swamp Pheasant (*Centropus phasianinus*) in the extensive cane fields of Queensland. Formerly an inhabitant of the dry scrub and grassland country it was an uncommon species, but since it has colonized the cane fields it is now said to be fairly plentiful. They are useful birds as they destroy small vermin and insects. In the West Indies the Orange-cheeked Waxbill (*Estrilda melpoda*), a species introduced from Africa, has colonized the canefields and adjoining pastures of Puerto Rico.

With the exception of the shifting cultivations of the Amerindian and other forest tribes, who move on when the land has lost its growing power, cultivations are seldom yielded to nature, with the consequent loss of food to birds. In any case, abandoned cultivations in the forest give rise to dense secondary growth, which provides more food and habitat than the original cultivations. An abandoned cultivation in the grassland areas usually takes on an appearance that resembles the adjoining untouched land, and is therefore not lost to birds unless through mismanagement it has become a dust bowl.

THE VISITORS TO THE TROPICS

Birds migration takes many forms and the extent of the journeys varies considerably. There are local migrations to find food and water within the tropics. Others actually cross the equatorial region from the temperate north to the south, from Europe to South Africa, for instance. But here we are only concerned with the species which breed in the temperate regions and visit the tropics during the winter months.

Until fairly recent times it was widely believed that the Swallow (*Hirundo rustica*), Cuckoo (*Cuculus canorus*), Wood Warbler (*Phylloscopus sibilatrix*) and Nightingale (*Luscinia megarhynchos*) hibernated like some mammals during the cold months, and emerged from the mud at the bottom of pools at the first hint of spring. Now it is known that these birds make long migrations to benefit from living in two widely separated regions. This involves moving from the regions where they nest and rear their young to their winter quarters where a plentiful supply of food is available, and where the climate is favourable and the hours of daylight are not

Golden Plover (Pacific race), Arctic Tern (*top*) and Red-necked Phalarope (*bottom right*)

reduced. Strangely, they always nest in the coldest part of their range, but there is also a plentiful supply of food in the spring, of course, and even more daylight hours for finding the food needed for their young.

Medium and long distance migration is related to climate, and the times and destinations of migration are for the most part constant. Birds usually return to the same locality year after year, unless blown off course, and often to the same nesting site. The ringing of Swallows has revealed that they return to the same building every year for nesting, after a journey of perhaps 8,000 kilometres (5,000 miles) each way. Stores of fat are laid down to provide energy for migratory flights, but on such long journeys they must feed *en route*. Some birds make sea crossings of up to 3,200 kilometres (2,000 miles), however, and could not possibly feed on the journey. The American Golden Plover (*Pluvialis dominica*), for example, flies non-stop from the mainland to Hawaii, and the tiny Ruby-throated Hummingbird (*Archilochus colubris*) migrates across the Gulf of Mexico to South America non-stop, a journey of 800 kilometres (500 miles).

Ruby-throated Hummingbird (*top left*), House Swallow (*top right*) and Chiffchaff

On long overland journeys halts of one or several days are usually made *en route*, although it has been reliably reported that flights across the Sahara may be made non-stop, and owing to bad weather conditions may take two days. Most birds fly for about eight hours in every twenty-four, covering perhaps 640 kilometres (400 miles) in that time.

Compared with the migration flights of northern species to the tropics and back there is relatively little bird migration from the southern hemisphere to the tropics, but then there is a vast difference in the extent of the temperate land masses in the hemispheres.

During storms and fog birds get lost on their flights, and the evidence suggests that they use the sun and stars to plot their course; but they must also be able to take drift into account by using landmarks, and to compensate for the changing position of the heavenly bodies when their journeys take several days. With the use of radar it has been possible to track migrating birds, and it has been shown that over England at least they travel at an altitude of about 950 metres (3,000 feet). Migration from eastern Europe and northern and

Migration. The map shows distances travelled by the shortest route, not necessarily the actual route followed.

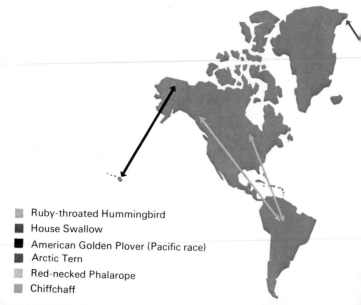

Ruby-throated Hummingbird
House Swallow
American Golden Plover (Pacific race)
Arctic Tern
Red-necked Phalarope
Chiffchaff

central Asia to the tropics mainly follows two routes through the Indus and Brahmaputra River valleys at either end of the Himalayan chain to southern India and Ceylon. Himalayan mountaineers have encountered birds, particularly waterfowl, passing directly over the mountain range also, at heights of 4,600 metres (15,000 feet). Some of these birds make non-stop flights too; the Woodcock (*Scolopax rusticola*) of northern Asia apparently does so on its flight to southern India.

Forty per cent of all Palearctic breeding species leave the region for warmer climes during the autumn. The birds of the eastern part of this region follow routes down the Malay peninsula, and even further east, into South East Asia and extending into Indonesia, the south west Pacific area, and Australasia. Others veer to the west and visit India. Some of these species are believed to use the Philippines as a land-bridge on their way to Borneo, and some passage migrants to places further south also use this route.

In East Africa a number of non-breeding birds, particularly waders, stay in the area during the breeding season in the colder northern spring.

Some highly insectivorous birds

Indian Paradise Flycatcher

Yellow-bellied Wattle-Eye

Scarlet-breasted Shrike

Green-billed Malcoha

BIRDS AND MAN IN THE TROPICS

Birds indirectly useful to man

But for the birds the world would perish is a phrase that has been repeated many times, and nowhere is it more appropriate than in the tropics where the temperature, and in some areas the humidity, provides an ideal all-year-round breeding ground for multitudes of insects. It has been estimated that a single pair of beetles of the prolific Chrysomelidae family could increase to 60,000,000 in one season if they were not checked; and butterfly and moth larvae can eat double their own weight of leaves daily. So there is good reason for keeping these insects in check, and birds do this admirably.

In many of the drier areas of Africa and south west Asia the most troublesome of the insect pests are the locusts; agriculturists dread the approach of their migrating hordes, as these can mean the difference between reasonable living or famine over a large area. Birds are the most effective natural check of the locusts, and many live exclusively upon them. In Ethiopia large flocks of Wattled Starlings (*Creatophora cinerea*) follow the locusts, and when these find a suitable egg-laying region the starlings nest also, and are assured of a good supply of 'hopper' locusts for their young.

A German ornithologist has estimated that a pair of titmice (Paridae) and their progeny eat 150,000 caterpillars and pupae annually; and the rapid growth of most birds is due to the fact that they consume more than their own weight of food for the first few days of their lives. Some nesting birds have been observed to bring insects to their young as many as 300 times daily; even the seed-eating birds feed their young on insects for the first few days, and many fruit-eaters do also.

Not only do birds prey upon the vegetarian insects, but also upon the disease vectors such as mosquitos and blowflies. Egrets and Sun Bitterns (*Eurypyga helias*) are adept at catching flies with a quick stab of their sharp bills, and a captive Gold-fronted Chloropsis (*Chloropsis aurifrons*) has been seen to catch and eat thirty-seven large blowflies within the space of ten minutes.

In addition to the insect-eating birds those which feed upon

Pariah Kite

Red-headed Merlin

Caracara

Spotted Eagle Owl

114

rodents are also useful to mankind, and the birds of prey are one of nature's most effective controls of the vermin hordes. Not only do these animals damage stored produce and growing crops, but they can also carry diseases that can be fatal to man. In theory a pair of rats producing eight babies six times annually could increase to about 900 in one year, assuming that the offspring commenced breeding when they were about three months old. Unchecked, the progeny of a single pair could result in over 900,000 million in five years. Fortunately they are checked: by many mammalian and reptilian predators and by natural disasters, and by the many species of birds that feed largely, and sometimes almost solely, upon rats and mice.

The large owls, for example, can eat at least two rats per day, a total of 1,500 every year for each pair. The Red-headed Merlin (*Falco chicquera*) of the dry Indian plains is a typical rodent eater. So is the larger Crested Serpent Eagle (*Spilornis cheela*) which inhabits wooded country. But so often these birds, whether diurnal or nocturnal hunters, are accused of taking domestic animals and are slaughtered on sight. From the facts given above it is quite obvious that this is a short-sighted policy, as even one chicken per week could not repay them for their work.

Rodent-eating is not restricted to the birds of prey, however. Many other carnivorous birds and even insectivorous species feed upon rats and mice in various stages of growth. In Africa the large Ground Hornbills (*Bucorvus abyssinicus*), in Australia the Kookaburra and in South America the Jabiru Stork include rodents in their daily diet. Even relatively small birds such as the shrikes (Laniidae) tackle mice, and have the gruesome habit of impaling them on thorns to eat later, which has earned them the popular name of 'butcher birds'. Throughout the tropics jays, magpies, treepies, storks, herons and many other birds catch and eat rodents whenever the opportunity presents itself.

Birds also act as seed dispersers and flower pollinators, and in the tropics where many groups of nectivorous birds occur they are almost as important as the insects in cross-pollinating certain plants. With the exception of a few nectar-seekers, the Diglossa for example, which pierces the side of the corolla

Black-naped Fruit Pigeon (*foreground*) and Knysna Touraco

to reach the nectar, many have special adaptations to enable them to reach the nectar from the front of the flower. Inserting their heads into the flowers the birds come into contact with the pollen-laden anthers, which deposit a small amount on the bird's feathers. This is then transferred to the stigma of the next mature female flower that the bird visits. In South America the hummingbirds and honeycreepers feed upon nectar and the small insects attracted to flowers, while in Africa and Asia the sunbirds and white-eyes (Zosteropidae) perform the same function. But many other birds sip nectar from flowers.

The wind and water mechanisms of seed dispersal are well known, but the seeds of many plants would merely drop to the ground and germinate there if it were not for the birds. The seeds of small berries that are swallowed whole are passed through the digestive tract unharmed and germinate whenever they fall upon suitable ground. In India the success of the sandalwood industry has been attributed to the bulbuls (Pycnonotidae), and the mulberry owes its abundance in some areas to bird propagation.

The large gapes of the fruit pigeons and touracos have already been mentioned, together with their ability to swallow large drupes and pass the stones out intact. Many fruit pigeons feed regularly upon the produce of the nutmeg tree, and the stones have been transported from island to island in Indonesia by these birds. Migrating birds carry seeds for long distances and assist the spread of plants. Ducks carry the seeds of water plants, and some have been found to have a higher germination rate after passing through the birds' intestines than seeds not treated in this way. The germination prospects of seeds swallowed by birds depend upon the length of time that they take to pass through the alimentary canal. Some birds even have modifications that enable stones, pips or seeds to pass through very quickly.

Cardinal Honeyeater (*left*) and Guiana Frilled Coquette Hummingbird

Scarlet-backed Flowerpecker (*top*) and Thick-billed Flowerpecker

Birds troublesome to man

The dispersal of seeds and cross-pollination of flowers by birds is not always economically beneficial, unfortunately. The fast-growing lantana weed was introduced into Ceylon early last century and has colonized many areas, and parts of India too. Many species of birds have helped to spread this pest by eating its glutinous berries, which are produced in great quantity and germinate quickly after passing unharmed through the birds' digestive tracts. The flowerpeckers (Dicaeidae) even have a modified intestine that allows them to feed upon the berries of the mistletoes that abound throughout forested southern Asia. The berries are swallowed whole and the sticky seeds are passed out and adhere to trees where they rapidly germinate. Sunbirds also assist in spreading these destructive plants by pollinating their flowers.

Some birds act as hosts or merely carriers of diseases that can affect the health of man and his domestic animals. Newcastle disease, for example, one of the most effective killers of domestic fowl, has been proved to be carried by wild birds that were seemingly unaffected by it. But it is as crop pests that some birds do tremendous damage, often causing famine through their ravages. In South East Asia several species of munias (Estrildidae) play havoc with the rice crops; and the Long-tailed Munia (*Erythrura prasina*) arrives in Borneo in great flocks every year just as the rice is ripening. It is interesting to note that they cannot have been pests of rice crops in Borneo for very long, as Tom Harrisson, for many years Curator of the Sarawak Museum, says that the ethnological evidence suggests that until fairly recently the basic carbohydrate food of the people was sago.

In the drier grassland areas of Africa the Black-crowned Waxbills (*Estrilda nonnula*) congregate in their thousands on the ripe millet, as do numerous other species of small seed-eating birds. In fact it is true to say that all seed and fruit crops in the tropics are attacked at some stage of their development by birds.

The damage the weavers and waxbills cause to seed crops in Africa is negligible compared with the devastation wrought

Long-tailed Munias feeding on rice

by another small bird, no larger than a sparrow. Whole regions have been famine stricken and the cultivation of crops favourable to the species has ceased in some areas. The Red-billed Quelea or Dioch (*Quelea quelea*) is the reason, and it has reached plague proportions in many parts of its range. It is a colonial nesting bird, and often occurs in flocks of over 1,000,000, with so many nests per tree that the combined weight has brought limbs, and in some cases the whole tree, to the ground. They are migratory birds, and seek corn crops from just south of the Sahara down into South Africa. It has been calculated that each Quelea will eat, or damage through pecking at the germ 56 grams (2 ounces) of wheat per day, and a million-strong flock can destroy over 50 tons daily.

In Central Tanganyika in 1890 the millet crop was so devasted by these birds that famine resulted and thereafter millet was replaced by sorghum. But this is as eagerly accepted and many crops have since been ruined. In the Transvaal in 1953 the European farmers alone lost sorghum valued at £500,000, and in the Sudan the crops have been destroyed so often that many farmers no longer grow sorghum, which was their staple diet. Wheat crops have been badly hit also; recently 100,000 bags were lost in Kenya in one year. Rice too – every grain on 9·5 hectares (24 acres) in West Africa was cleared within a few days some years ago.

The species has few natural enemies, and the birds are so mobile and colonial in their habits that within a very short time they can breed many miles from an area where they have been disturbed. In recent years the increased water supplies and the development of marginal land has reduced the need for them to make migratory flights in search of food and water, and, if anything, has increased their rate of multiplication. In attempts to reduce their numbers they have been sprayed with poison and their nest sites have been dynamited or destroyed with flame-throwers, but still they persist. Recently in Tanzania over 80,000,000 queleas were destroyed in two years, and in West Africa 124,000,000 were killed in one year.

Attempting to control Red-billed Queleas by burning their nests; male in foreground

Although it has been severely persecuted the Emu has survived the influx of settlers and their introduced animals into Australia, and still thrives in many areas, often to the extent of being a pest. It is found throughout the continent except in the forests of the extreme north, but it is mainly a nuisance in the wheat-growing areas just below the Tropic of Capricorn. In the wheat country of Western Australia it is even classed as vermin, and serious efforts have been made to control its numbers. In 1932 a detachment of the Royal Australian Artillery was sent to engage 20,000 Emus that were feeding in the wheatlands, but the birds dispersed into small units and the machine-gunners, who were not equipped for guerilla warfare, were forced to withdraw.

Fruit crops fare little better than cereal in some regions. In India large flocks of Ring-necked Parakeets (*Psittacula krameri*) and the similar but larger Alexandrine Parakeets (*Psittacula eupatria*) attack ripening fruit with their large bills. In common with most members of the parrot family they are probably the most wasteful of all birds, and damage far more

Emus in wheat field

than they eat.

In addition to the crop pests there are the pests of domestic livestock, although they are not pests or vermin in the true sense of the word, but are so labelled because they may occasionally take poultry, calves, lambs or goat kids. The majority of the larger tropical birds of prey have been included in this category at one time, and all too frequently they are destroyed on sight. Wild animals are, of course, the basic diet of all these birds, and they are essential to maintain a correct balance between the predator and prey species. The African Goshawk (*Accipiter tachiro*) is a particularly rapacious bird and even attacks poultry in the suburbs of large towns, so its presence is seldom tolerated. Even the Osprey has been killed in many parts of its range because it competes with the fisherman. In India the Tawny Eagle (*Aquila rapax*), the commonest eagle in the country, is said to become troublesome to poultry when it is rearing its young, whereas it is normally a scavenger, and as such is a useful bird.

African Goshawk attacking a domestic hen

Indian Mynah

Spotted Dove

Orange-cheeked Waxbill

House Sparrow

Introduced birds

In the temperate regions exotic birds have often been introduced to increase the supplies of game birds for shooting, but introductions into the tropics have mainly been of passerines, and often for such simple reasons as to form a 'link with home'. No thought was given to the fact that introduced birds might compete with the indigenous birds or damage native plants. Fortunately, many deliberate introductions were unsuccessful, and it has since been shown that birds only became naturalized in areas where the conditions corresponded with their natural habitat. The House Sparrow (*Passer domesticus*), a native of Europe, North Africa and parts of Asia, has now doubled its world range as a result of intentional and accidental introductions, and now inhabits over one quarter of the earth's land area. In the tropics it has been introduced into South America, Hawaii and New Caledonia and to Jamaica, Cuba and St. Thomas in the West Indies.

The Starling (*Sturnus vulgaris*) is also widespread from Grand Bahama Island to the Pacific Ocean islands. The Bahama race of the West Indian Red-bellied Woodpecker (*Centurus superciliaris*) is now very rare, owing, it is thought, to the Starlings which nest in the woodpecker holes. The Starling and House Sparrow have done so well in cultivated areas in the tropics because they were adapted to living in a similar sort of habitat in their native countries, and were able to oust indigenous species as a result of their higher degree of specialization for life in this niche. All exotic species that have become established have either taken over a vacant niche, which is hardly likely in most cases, or they have usurped native birds.

Two groups of islands, the Seychelles and Hawaiian islands, have been colonized by the Common Mynah (*Acridotheres tristis*), introduced from India. On the Seychelles they compete with the Magpie Robin (*Copsychus seychellarum*) which is now very rare, and on Hawaii the unique avifauna has also had to contend with the introduced white-eye, whose presence has undoubtedly affected the last Hawaiian Nukupuus (*Hemignathus lucidus*), a species of honeycreeper. Throughout the tropics there are examples of competition between native and exotic birds, usually to the detriment of the native species.

In addition to damaging habitat and native birds, introduced species have also been injurious to crops. Starlings and mynahs eat soft fruits and surprisingly the House Sparrow has also been labelled a crop pest in India. The noted ornithologist Salim Ali has referred to this bird as the most familiar species in India, both in the forest hamlets and bustling cities and in the hills and plains where enormous flocks damage ripening crops.

There have been instances, however, where birds have been introduced into new lands for conservation reasons. One of the earliest of these projects was the translocation of a number of Greater Birds of Paradise (*Paradisaea apoda*) from New Guinea to the island of Little Tobago in the West Indies. Sir William Ingram purchased the island in 1909 as a sanctuary for this species as he considered that it faced extinction in its native land. He sponsored an expedition to the Aru Islands, adjoining New Guinea, and forty-eight

Common Starlings damaging peach crop

specimens were collected and subsequently released on Little Tobago. On Sir William's death the small island was handed over to the British Government as a permanent sanctuary for the species. Thickly forested and less than 170 metres (550 feet) high, the habitat was ideal for the Greater Bird of Paradise, a lowland species, whereas so many kinds of these birds are restricted to the mountain forests. For many years the numbers remained constant at about two dozen, undoubtedly the ceiling for this limited habitat, until a severe hurricane hit the island some years ago and reduced both the forest habitat and the birds.

Recently the West Indies has been the scene of another translocation operation, but on this occasion it was birds' eggs that were moved, from Trinidad's Caroni Swamp to the Everglades in Florida. The eggs were those of the Scarlet Ibis (*Eudocimus ruber*), and of the twenty-four that I collected the majority hatched later under their White Ibis (*E. albus*) foster parents in Florida, and the first stage of the introduction of Scarlet Ibises into a new, protected habitat was successful.

Greater Bird of Paradise displaying

127

Exploitation of birds

In 1880 a company was formed in Germany to exploit the resources of New Guinea, and in five years over 50,000 bird of paradise skins were exported. In 1911 the skin exports from Kaiser Wilhelm Land alone amounted to 7,000, and many species were endangered. Fortunately, however, the trade was prohibited before any were too severely affected, and Sir William Ingram's fears for the safety of the Greater Bird of Paradise did not materialize as the indications are that they recovered from the heavy cropping.

Civilized man has always demanded the skins of birds, or just their plumes, for ornamentation, and their flesh for the pot. The Little Egret (*Egretta garzetta*) was practically exterminated early this century for its long crest plumes and its 'aigrettes' – the filamentous feathers on its back and breast – for the millinery trade. Unfortunately for the species these feathers are part of the bird's breeding plumage, and as the adults were shot quite unrestrictedly during the nesting period many nestlings were left to die. At the height of the fashion craze some of the pressure on the wild birds was relieved by captive breeding, particularly in the Sind in India. But attempts to control the trade and the killing were of little avail as the stakes were high, and little thought was given by the hunters to the effects on the bird populations. Even a National Audubon Society warden was killed in Florida when trying to protect egrets from plume hunters.

Also at the turn of the century Ostrich plumes were in demand, but fortunately for the world's largest bird it was more economical to breed them in captivity. On the Ostrich farms, particularly in South Africa, it was possible to crop the plumes two or three times per year, but the demand slumped just after the First World War when feather boas went out of fashion. Even albatross feathers have been in demand, particularly on the Pacific islands. On Laysan Island in the Hawaiian group Japanese plumage hunters practically exterminated the breeding populations.

Killing for the pot has been even more damaging to some bird populations. The poor Dodo (*Raphus cucullatus*) is a typical example of a helpless bird that has been exterminated by man for food.

Little Egrets at nest

Although the external trade in bird of paradise skins is now illegal, a large internal trade still thrives between the tribes. Dance festivals still play an important part in the tribal life of the New Guinea highlanders, and the value of plumes on display at the massive annual dance held in the Wahgi Valley has been estimated to be £100,000. One of the side effects of contact between these tribesmen and the outside world is that they now have more money and, now that the inter-tribal warring has stopped, more time on their hands, so they can afford to buy more plumes, or guns to shoot their own birds. The result is that even tribes which do not use plumes for ceremonial purposes now trade in them. Several birds of paradise species are threatened as a result of this over-hunting for ceremonial plumes, and some highland tribes even have to import plumes from other areas as the birds in their own territory have been so drastically reduced.

The bare primary shafts of the large flightless cassowaries are highly valued by some highland tribes for use as nose-septums; and the birds' feathers are also used in head-dresses. Young cassowaries are often caught and reared, and are housed in stockades when adult and periodically relieved of their feathers. Their quills are bent into rings and used as ear ornaments. Tribesmen throughout the tropics use bird feathers for ornamentation. The Dyaks of Borneo incorporate the wing and tail feathers of the larger species of hornbills in their head-dresses and ceremonial cloaks. The most coveted feathers are the fine central tail retrices of the Helmeted Hornbill (*Rhinoplax vigil*), whose beak may also be used as an ear ornament. The feathers of the Argus Pheasant are used in Indonesia as decorations, and the primitive negritos of Malaya make use of feathers from the Green Peafowl (*Pavo muticus*) and Red Junglefowl (*Gallus gallus*).

In the New World macaw and toucan feathers are widely used by Amerindian tribes in their large head-dresses, but in Africa there is little use of feathers, possibly because of the wealth of mammalian skins, tails and horns for ornamentation, except for ceremonial crowns.

Feather crown of Swaziland incorporating red and violet touraco feathers and the drooping plumes of Jackson's Whydah

As well as the large scale killing of tropical birds for their skins and flesh, there is also a thriving trade in other bird products, although this is often conducted in a manner that does not affect the viability of the wild populations. In western Borneo, for instance, particularly in the great caves of Niah, large numbers of cave swiftlets (*Collocalia* spp.) nest. Like the larger swifts (Apodidae) they construct their nests with a secretion of their salivary glands to bind the materials together, but they use more cement and less fibre. The nests of the Grey-rumped Swiftlets (*Collocalia francica*) are made from almost pure salivary secretion, which sets hard. These nests have been cropped for generations by the Chinese for making the famed birds' nest soup. Rigid rules control the welfare of the caves and the nesting birds, and it is the duty of the Curator of the Sarawak Museum to decide when nest collection will take place, and the extent of the crop.

Guano – accumulated bird droppings – is also collected from the caves for use as fertilizer, but it is on the Pacific 'bird coast' of South America that bird guano has become a product of international trade. On the Peruvian coast and its neighbouring islands the Peruvian Cormorant or Guanay (*Phalacrocorax bougainvillii*), the Brown Pelican (*Pelecanus occidentalis*) and the Peruvian Booby (*Sula variegata*) nest in their millions. The arid climate has preserved their droppings and, more important, has not leached them of their nitrogen content, so that they are a highly nutritious plant food.

First collected by the Incas, guano was harvested throughout Spanish colonial rule, but did not become a commercial proposition until von Humboldt saw its economic value. Although the Incas had carefully controlled guano cropping most Peruvians could think only of the removal of as much as possible, and between 1848 and 1875 over twenty million tons were exported as fertilizer. Many islands were reduced to bedrock and early this century Peruvian agriculture was threatened with disaster through the lack of fertilizer. At last the birds were protected and the removal of their guano was strictly controlled. Slowly a return to large-scale harvesting has been possible.

Collecting nests of the Grey-rumped Swiftlet (*inset*) in Borneo

Although they still rely upon wild animals for their protein supplies many Amerindian tribes of South America are inveterate pet keepers, and they do not restrict themselves to the dogs which they use when hunting. Shooting with blowpipe, bow and arrow and recently old shotguns, mammals provide the bulk of their animal food, but birds also fall to their missiles. Even such bizarre birds as the cocks of the rock (*Rupicola* spp.) are killed. If, however, the hunters find tinamou, guan, trumpeter or curassow chicks they take them back to their villages and rear them. Nor do they limit this inborn ability to rearing precocial chicks, for they also care for young tanagers, hangnests, toucans, parrots and macaws. These bird pets are seldom used for the pot when mature, and with the exception of the cage birds they wander freely around the villages. In times of war between the tribes trumpeters (Psophiidae) were often used as watchdogs, and their booming call would awaken the tribesmen when danger threatened.

The young of the hole-nesting parrots and macaws are acquired when trees are chopped down for building purposes or for making canoes, and it is the normal practice to 'mouthfeed' these young birds with chewed cassava bread and banana, just as the parent birds would feed them. They are also allowed their liberty when independent, but they seldom move far from the vicinity of the village. Tanagers and other small cage birds are kept in woven baskets which hang under the eaves of the huts. The 'captive' bird life of a remote Akawaio village in the Pacaraima Mountains that I visited some years ago was typical of many in the area. It included a Red and Blue Macaw (*Ara chloroptera*), baby Blue Tanagers (*Thraupis episcopus*) and a Black-throated Oriole (*Icterus nigrogularis*) in a basket; and among the many dogs and children lived a group of trumpeters, a pair of Little Chachalacas (*Ortalis motmot*) and a curassow. During the days I lived in the village Hahn's Macaws (*Ara nobilis*), Blackheaded Caiques (*Pionites melanocephala*) and some young toucans were also brought in.

American Indian encampment with Blue and Yellow Macaw, Blue Tanager (in cage), Giant Razor-billed Curassow (*bottom left*) and White-winged Trumpeter

Every year thousands of tropical birds are imported into the British Isles, North America and Europe, mainly for the pet trade. In 1966 266,000 cage birds entered the United States, and in the same year India exported over 1,750,000 birds. Many others are shipped from Africa, South East Asia and South America, particularly from Ecuador. Fortunately, many countries have recently revised their laws governing the exportation of wild birds, and they will certainly not be shipped in such large numbers in the future. Other countries have restricted the numbers which can be caught for some years, and some – Trinidad and Kenya, for example – only allow indigenous birds to be exported to bona fide zoological gardens. All native birds are protected in Australia, and only those which are genuinely surplus to zoos can be exported legally, and then only to non-commercial zoos.

Talking birds have always been in great demand, and when the 'parrot ban' restricted the importation of parrots and their relatives into the British Isles for many years, the Greater Hill Mynah (*Gracula religiosa intermedia*) virtually replaced the parrot as the favourite talker.

Since the parrot import restrictions were removed the pet market has been flooded with these birds. Ring-necked (*Psittacula krameri*) and Blossom-headed Parakeets (*P. cyanocephala*) from India, amazon parrots and macaws from South America, and Senegal Parrots (*Poicephalus senegalus*) and African Grey Parrots (*Psittacus erithacus*) from West Africa have been imported in vast numbers. Many exporters offer reduced price incentives for dealers buying a hundred or more. Most of these species are easy to cater for, but many others – particularly the soft-billed birds – are very delicate and have specialized food requirements and feeding techniques. The losses involved in the trapping and shipping of these birds from their countries of origin are often very high, and it is not uncommon for seventy-five per cent losses *en route* to be experienced in consignments of delicate sunbirds and flowerpeckers sent from the Far East. It has been suggested that for every cage bird retailed to bird fanciers at least four will have died. The losses of the hardier seed-eating finches and waxbills before shipment and in transit are, of course, lower.

(*Above left to right*) Java Sparrow, Waxbill, Golden-crowned
Euphoria; (*below*) Hill Mynah (*left*) and Yellow-headed Amazon
Parrot

In recent years there has been a proliferation of zoos and bird gardens which also use tropical birds, although not in the numbers that are absorbed annually by the pet trade. Basically the demand is for a limited number of the kinds of bird that are in demand as pets, such as the smaller soft-bills and seed-eaters, plus parrots, birds of prey, waterfowl, pheasants, waders, pelicans, cranes, storks, the large flightless birds and many others. These large birds have a longer life span than most 'pet' birds of the cage bird type, with the exception, of course, of the parrots. Consequently the replacement factor is low if good animal husbandry is practised. However complete a collection is, certain birds are always in demand and Harpy Eagles (*Harpia harpyja*), Wattled Cranes (*Bugeranus carunculatus*), Ocellated Turkeys (*Agriocharis ocellata*) and umbrella birds (*Cephalopterus* spp.) are eagerly sought by the establishments which can afford them. In addition to being impressive and long-lived, many of these birds are very hardy even though tropical in origin. Once acclimatized they thrive in sub-zero temperatures and do not need elaborate heated accommodation. It is not uncommon these days to see toucans, Scarlet Ibises and even hummingbirds bathing in their outside aviaries when there is snow on the ground, although the latter birds do need heated indoor quarters.

There are restrictions on the exportation of certain birds from their native lands, but with the exception of members of the waterfowl and pheasant families which have to be quarantined, birds can be imported quite openly into the British Isles for exhibition purposes. There is a large trade in flamingos, and most establishments have a sizeable flock of several species, including the rare high altitude Andean ones. All flamingo owners endeavour to produce the most natural-looking bird, and provide foodstuffs designed to supply the carotenoid pigment necessary to retain the delicate pink or red shading of their feathers.

The emphasis these days in zoos and bird gardens is on the provision of suitable accommodation. The old type of completely artificial bird-cage is unfortunately still in

Hyacinthine Macaw (*left*) and Indian Peacock

evidence, but many new establishments are creating planted, landscaped compartments which are in effect bird habitats.

Man has been able to control the breeding and maintenance of a number of wild birds over a long period, and has altered most of them morphologically to improve their economic and, in some instances, their aesthetic value. The distinguishing features necessary for domestication were a digestive system tolerant of replacement – and often completely artificial – diets, reproductive behaviour which could easily be moulded to captive life, and the acceptance of the proximity of man.

To provide eggs and flesh several species of gallinaceous birds and waterfowl have been domesticated. The Red Jungle-fowl (*Gallus gallus*) is usually considered to be the ancestor of our domestic fowl, and its domestication is believed to have commenced in India about 3,000 years B.C., and it appeared in China and the Middle East 1,500 years later. From this bird heavy meat breeds such as the Brahma, light egg-laying breeds such as the White Leghorn, and dual purpose breeds such as the Rhode Island Red have been derived, and in addition numerous fancy breeds.

Of the other gallinaceous birds that are now an accepted part of our way of living, the turkeys originated in the New World, where the Mexican subspecies of the Wild Turkey

Muscovy Duck: wild (*left*) and domestic forms

(*Meleagris gallopavo*) gave rise to the Norfolk Blacks and Beltsville Whites. They were originally thought to have come from Eastern Europe, hence their name. The Peafowl that are now so common in parks and the gardens of stately homes, are domesticated from the Blue Peafowl (*Pavo cristatus*) of India, and although there have been no changes in size or shape, the black-shouldered, pied and white forms have been developed.

Morphological differences of size, shape, plumage and even skin colour have also been produced in ducks, together with physiological differences of increased egg production, food conversion, for example, although to a lesser extent than in the fowl breeds. With the exception of the Muscovy (*Cairina moschata*), domestic ducks are derived from the widespread Mallard (*Anas platyrhynchos*). It is believed that they were first domesticated in South East Asia long ago. Apart from its colour the Muscovy Duck is little different from the wild bird which occurs in South America.

Domestic geese are also thought to have originated in South East Asia from the Greylag Goose (*Anser anser*), with the exception of the Chinese Goose, a domestic breed derived from the wild Swan Goose (*A. cygnoides*).

Jungle Fowl (*foreground*) and domestic fowl

THE ASSOCIATION OF BIRDS WITH OTHER ANIMALS IN THE TROPICS

Birds mainly associate with mammals to benefit from the insect pests which they have on their bodies, or from the insects disturbed by the mammals, particularly in grasslands. The Cattle Egret (*Bubulcus ibis*) is practically cosmopolitan in the tropics and is often referred to as the 'Tick Bird' because it associates with the large herbivores, both domestic and wild, and gathers the insects disturbed by them. It also picks ticks off resting animals and can frequently be seen riding on the backs of moving ones. They even associate with man too, and follow tractors over newly ploughed land.

The 'Crocodile Bird' – the Egyptian Plover (*Pluvianus aegyptius*) – also performs a similar function to the Cattle Egrets, but on basking crocodiles. It feeds on their external parasites, a habit that has also been recorded for some Common Sandpipers (*Actitis hypoleucos*), but the Crocodile Bird's practice of picking leeches and decaying food particles from crocodiles' open mouths, apparently first recorded by Herodotus, has few reliable records to authenticate it. The Water Dikkop (*Burhinus vermiculatus*), a large plover-like bird, nests within a few feet of crocodile nests, apparently for the protection afforded them from the attacks of other predators.

When the birds and their host animals both benefit from the association it is known as commensalism, and many birds derive the bulk of their food from this habit. The oxpeckers certainly do, and the two species – Yellow-billed (*Buphagus africanus*) and the Red-billed (*B. erythrorhynchus*) – perch on all the African game animals with the exception of the elephant to feed upon the ticks on their hides and scar tissue, flesh and blood from their wounds. They have been welcomed for the part they play in clearing domestic animals of disease-harbouring parasites, but have also been accused of transmitting disease by feeding on the blood of an infected animal and soon afterwards on a healthy individual. They are well adapted for their job, with sharp claws for clinging on to and running along a beast, and a flattened, sharp-edged bill for scissoring off ticks and flesh.

In West Africa the Piapiac (*Ptilostomus afer*), a glossy

Oxpeckers on rhinoceros ; Cattle Egrets in grass

Ratel and man following a Honeyguide

black and brown bird resembling a magpie, associates in a similar way with domestic and wild animals, often riding on the backs of sheep and goats in the native villages. It is even tolerated by the elephants, which will never permit oxpeckers to seek parasites on their bodies.

Amphibious mammals also have their attendant birds, and both cormorants and Crab Plovers (*Dromas ardeola*) have been seen on the backs of partly submerged hippopotamuses. It is thought that they seek insects there, although they may just have been using the hippos as resting places or as vantage points when seeking food. Hammerheads (*Scopus umbretta*) are also said to do this when searching for frogs.

In the tropical forests birds often follow bands of monkeys through the tree tops and catch the insects disturbed by them. In West Africa the White-crested Hornbill (*Tropicranus albocristatus*), one of the most insectivorous species, regularly follows monkey troops; and this behaviour has also been recorded for the Fairy Bluebird (*Irena puella*) in the Philippines and several species of drongos (Dicruridae) in Asia.

The most unusual association between birds and other animals, including man, is shown by the honeyguides (Indicatoridae). They are insectivorous birds, and two of the species have developed a liking for bee larvae and beeswax. They cannot possibly obtain this food on their own and have developed the habit of guiding ratels or honey badgers to a wild bees' nest. After the nest has been opened up and robbed they are able to feed on the larvae and wax. With the arrival of man, who because of his liking for honey has to a certain extent substituted himself for the ratel, the honeyguide now attracts either man or ratel to the nest. When it has discovered a nest the honeyguide makes itself known by calling and fanning its tail, and when it has attracted the attention of a potential foraging partner it keeps about 5·5 metres (6 yards) ahead until the nest is reached. There is now apparently evidence that the more sophisticated Africans are no longer interested in wild honey and the honeyguides are less inclined to attract man to bees' nests. As an adaptation to their peculiar diet they have thick skins as a defence against bee stings. One of the two guiding species, the Black-throated Honeyguide has the name of *Indicator indicator*.

Temminck's Tragopan

BIRDS IN DANGER

Many birds are food for other animals, and in addition to their natural losses through predation large numbers are taken for food by the hunting tribes. In recent years, however, birds throughout the tropics have been threatened by the predations of 'civilized' man.

The future of the Grey Junglefowl (*Gallus sonneratii*) is in jeopardy as a result of over-killing merely for its feathers, as these are highly regarded by fishing-fly manufacturers. India has banned their exportation but they are still smuggled out by way of Nepal and Pakistan. Also in southern Asia Blythe's Tragopan (*Tragopan blythi*) of the forested regions of Burma and Assam, is now rare in the wild state because it has been hunted for food, and unlike many of the ornamental pheasants it is barely represented in captivity.

Birds of localized distribution suffer more than most, particularly in remote regions where the enforcement of protection laws is a difficult task, and it is quite likely that several more species will follow the localized Pink-headed Duck (*Rhodonessa caryophyllacea*) into extinction as a result of man's predations. In the forests of West Africa live the two species of unique Rockfowl: the Grey-necked species (*Picathartes oreas*) in the Cameroon and the White-necked Rockfowl (*Picathartes gymnocephalus*) which has a limited distribution from Sierra Leone to Togo. Little was known of the habits of either species until fairly recently, when it was found that they breed only on rocky outcrops deep in the jungle. As they are very localized and their nest sites are now well known to the natives, they have been continually worried over the last decade for museum and zoo specimens.

Large well-fleshed birds are shot for the pot wherever they occur, but the gunners do not always restrict themselves to shooting during open seasons. Even Scarlet Ibises have been poached in their protected nesting colonies. Many birds of prey are thoughtlessly killed because of their predations or supposed predations on domestic stock, or because man feels that he has prior claim on their natural foods. The Hawaiian

Hawaiian O-O and Bare-headed Rockfowl (*bottom*)

Hawk (*Buteo solitarius*), the Galapagos Hawk (*Buteo galapagoensis*) and Reunion Harrier (*Circus maillardi maillardi*) have all suffered in this way and are now rare birds.

During this century and particularly in the last two decades millions of acres of land have been improved in the tropics. At least, from man's point of view they have been improved, to grow more crops for the ever increasing human population, but for many species of birds it is a form of destruction with which they cannot possibly cope. They have evolved to life in their particular habitat over many years, in some cases millions, and they cannot change in the course of half a century. Marshes are being drained, or at least controlled and converted into paddy fields. Vast areas of forest have been cleared for the paper mills and furniture manufacturers, and the grasslands have been tilled to provide grain for the masses.

Some birds can adapt to this change of habitat and diet. Many of the African seed-eaters are content to eat cultivated grain instead of the wild seeds and, if anything, are increasing because of the more abundant food supplies. Also the cultivated areas tend to favour some of the introduced birds which were adapted to life in such a habitat in their native lands. But these species are in the minority and for every example

Great Bustard

of birds which can adapt there are several of birds that are now threatened with extinction because of the loss of their habitat.

In the Hawaiian islands many highly specialized endemic birds have been reduced and some exterminated because of the destruction of their forest habitat, particularly the loss of the mature trees on which the Hawaiian honeycreepers were dependent for their food. In Ceylon the Red-faced Malcoha (*Phaenicophaeus pyrrhocephalus*) is now restricted to the few remaining areas of dense jungle that remain in the central province. The Great Indian Bustard (*Ardeotis nigriceps*) was once plentiful in the sparse grasslands and scrub plains, but these are now being claimed for cultivating and the species has been reduced to danger level.

The case of the Hook-billed Kite (*Chondrohierax uncinatus*) of Cuba is both unique and unfortunate, as it proves how reliant some species are upon their habitat. This species is now in danger because the reduction of the forests has reduced the availability of the tree snails on which it feeds.

In general the birds restricted to relatively small islands

have suffered most at the hands of man, and many species have been exterminated through his exploitation, thoughtlessness and lack of care. When bird populations are reduced in part of a niche it is normal for others of the same species to repopulate the vacant area, provided the habitat is undisturbed. The small niches of tropical islands have been unable to provide these replacements for any length of time, when there has been continual harrassment of the total populations. In addition to over-hunting and destruction of their habitat there are innumerable instances of the existence of insular species being threatened by introduced predators.

The Whip-poor-will of Puerto Rico (*Caprimulgus noctitherus*) which was thought to have been extinct since the end of the last century – happily it was rediscovered in 1961 – is believed to have declined as a result of predation by the introduced Indian Mongoose; and these vicious little carnivores have also taken their toll of the White-breasted Thrasher (*Ramphocinclus brachyurus*) of Martinique and numerous other endemic West Indian species. The mongooses were introduced to combat the plagues of rats on several islands, but when the rats took to the trees to escape them they found a new supply of food ready for the taking. On other islands introduced rats have been an endless source of trouble to the native birds, particularly the ground-nesting species. The Tahiti Flycatcher

White-headed Curassow

Imperial Amazon Parrot (*left*) and Wattled False Sunbird

(*Pomarea nigra*) has been reduced by them, and in New Caledonia the Kagu (*Rhynochetus jubatus*) had little defence against them, and the introduced cats, dogs and pigs. The Kagu has of course evolved in a 'Garden of Eden' in the absence of predators, and is virtually flightless and nests on the ground. It now only occurs in the most remote mountainous areas.

There have been many other examples of cats, rats, dogs and pigs, all introduced by man either accidentally or intentionally, destroying the endemic birds on small islands. The Galapagos islands have suffered, and Fiji, Jamaica and Samoa also. There has even been an instance of introduced monkeys exterminating an insular species: the St Christopher's Island race of the Puerto Rico Bullfinch (*Loxigilla porforicensis grandis*) was killed off by *Cercopithecus* monkeys. In the Hawaiian group the Laysan Finch-bill (*Psittirostra cantans*) was almost extirpated when introduced rabbits cleared most of the vegetation, but it managed to recover when an expedition eliminated the rabbits.

Lammergeyer

The present plight of many tropical birds is indeed a sorry one, and for some there is little that can be done to prevent their ultimate extermination. Drained marshes cannot, or will not, be recreated; the conscience-stricken planting of saplings cannot replace the mature flowering and fruiting trees necessary for some birds, nor will man's need for grain allow him to tolerate seed-eating birds in his crops.

The measures taken to ensure the survival of threatened birds include the establishment of sanctuaries and legislation to restrict their killing or exportation for zoos, as pets, or for other commercial purposes. Zoo organizations, on a national basis, are well aware of the plight of some species which are usually considered to be prize exhibits, and have agreed not to trade in them. The rare Monkey-eating Eagle (*Pithecophaga jefferyi*) of the Philippines is now 'protected' by this creditable agreement.

Bird protection obviously includes protection of their habitat. Two extreme examples of this are the legislation to prevent the cutting of reeds in Lake Atitlan in Guatemala where the Giant Pied-billed Grebe (*Podilymbus gigas*) lives; and the establishment of the Luquillo National Forest in Puerto Rico, where the islands only endemic parrot – the Puerto Rican Parrot (*Amazona vittata*) – is confined. Of course, it is one thing to grant protection to birds inside national parks, but it is not always an easy task to enforce the laws and patrol the areas. Birds protected outside national parks or reserves fare even worse, and the African Lammergeyer (*Gypaetus barbatus meridionalis*) of the mountainous regions of the eastern seaboard of that continent has suffered through irresponsible shooting and poisoning.

Many organizations exist to gather facts on endangered birds, and to collect funds and provide specialist information on birds which sorely need protection and the best means of undertaking it. One of the major difficulties in this work is stimulating interest and compassion for small, unknown birds on remote islands. Recently the International Council for Bird Preservation managed to negotiate the purchase of Cousin Island in the Seychelles, thereby ensuring the perpetuation of some of the world's rarest birds.

Breeding wild birds in zoological gardens, bird gardens

Rothschild's Grackle

153

Golden-shouldered Parrot

Swinhoe's Pheasant

and related establishments can also aid the conservation effort and, indeed, has been successful on many occasions in the past. There are large captive stocks of pheasants and waterfowl in these collections, and in the hands of numerous private breeders too. Some of these birds are very rare in the wild state, and yet breed fairly readily in captivity. Others are now unobtainable from their countries of origin, mainly for political reasons, and the present captive stocks have all been bred from the original importations that were made many years ago. Some species have even been returned to their native lands in an attempt to help the wild populations. The Swinhoe's Pheasant (*Lophura swinhoei*), for example, is rare in the mountain forests of Formosa, and a number of captive-bred birds have recently been returned to the island to help build up viable breeding stocks again. One of the additional benefits of such a translocation is that it draws attention to the state of wildlife far better than any outburst in print, and can result in legislation to protect the birds. The Néné or Hawaiian Goose (*Branta sandvicensis*) was reduced to a handful of specimens some years ago, but breeding efforts in that country, England and America have been so successful that 150 birds have been returned to the wild, and sanctuaries totalling 18,000 acres have been established for their continued propagation.

When birds are protected and are no longer available to aviculturists, there is an even greater incentive to breed from the existing captive stocks, and this is exactly what has happened in the case of the Australian grass parakeets (*Neophema* spp. and *Psephotus* spp.). Their plight in the wild state has been blamed on collecting for the pet trade, but since the banning of all Australian bird exports many young have been produced annually by private aviculturists, although the financial incentives cannot be disregarded.

Not only does the breeding of rare birds deserve acclaim. Many Ostriches, Emus and rheas are bred in the world's zoos annually, and while they are not rare in the wild state they are certainly being reduced as their habitat shrinks. To establish even larger groups of these birds, and others, is the aim of many establishments, in order to reduce the drain upon the wild stocks.

BOOKS TO READ

The following books are recommended for further reading and are usually available from bookshops and public libraries or can be obtained by them.

A New Dictionary of Birds edited by A. L. Thomson. Nelson, London, 1964

Birds of Borneo by B. E. Smythies. Oliver and Boyd, Edinburgh, 1960

Birds of Burma by B. E. Smythies. Oliver and Boyd, Edinburgh, 1953

Birds of Colombia by R. Meyer de Schauensee. Livingstone Publishing Company, Wynnewood, Pa.

Birds of Eastern and North eastern Africa, Series 1, Vols. 1 and 2, by C. W. Mackworth-Praed and C. H. B. Grant. Longmans

Birds of Surinam by F. Haverschmidt. Oliver and Boyd, Edinburgh, 1968

Birds of Trinidad and Tobago by G. A. C. Herklots. Collins, London, 1965

Birds of the West Indies by J. Bond. Collins, London, 1960

Birds of the World by P. Barruel. Harrap, London, 1961

Handbook of New Guinea Birds by A. L. Rand and E. T. Gilliard. Weidenfeld and Nicholson, London, 1967

Red Data Book, Vol. 2, *Aves* by J. Vincent. I.U.C.N., Morges, 1966

The Birds of the Malay Peninsula, Singapore and Penang by A. G. Glenister. Oxford University Press, London, 1951

The Birds of South America by R. Meyer de Schauensee. Livingstone Publishing Company, Wynnewood, Pa., 1971

The Birds of West and Equatorial Africa, Vols. 1 and 2, by D. A. Bannerman. Oliver and Boyd, Edinburgh, 1953

The Book of Indian Birds by Salim Ali. Bombay Natural History Society, Bombay, 1964

PLACES TO VISIT

Most zoos have special bird collections, many of which contain representative tropical species.

INDEX

Page numbers in bold type
refer to illustrations

Accipiter tachiro 123
Acridotheres tristis 125
Acrocephalus arundinaceus
  63
  luscinia rehsei 105
Acryllium volturinum 36
Actitis hypoleucos 58, 142
Actophilornis africanus 68,
  73, **73**
Adjutant 94
Aerocharis prevostii 93
Afropavo congensis 24-5,
  24
Agapornis roseicollis 42
Agelaius icterocephalus **104**
  106
Agriocharis ocellata 139
Alseonax adustus 101
Amaurornis phoenicurus
  105
Amazona spp. 54, 153
Ammomanes spp. 38
Anas platyrhynchos 141
Anastomus oscitans 61
Anser spp. 141
Anseranas semipalmata 61,
  62
Ant-pitta, Streak-chested
  23
Anthracothorax viridigula
  41, 42
Aplonis panayensis 97
Aquila rapax 123
Ara spp. 54, 135
Ardeola grayii 61
Ardeotis spp. 36, 46
Argusianus argus 83, **25**
Arola goliath **52**, 58-59
Asity, Velvety 93
Aspatha gularis 76
Attagis gayi 76
Avocet 64, **65**
Aythya fuligula 66

Balaenicips rex 58-59
Balearica pavonina **32**, 46
Banaquit **88**, 98
Barbets **9**, 13, **23**, **96**
Bee-eater, Carmine 44, **49**
Birds of Paradise 29, **86**
  126-127, **127**
Bishopbird, Red **43**
Bittern, Sun 57, 113
Bluebird, Fairy **90**, 145

Booby, Peruvian 133
Bowerbird, Golden **85**
Bradornis pallidus 101
Branta sandvicensis 155
Bubulcus ibis 71, **106**, 142
  143
Bucorvus abyssinicus 115
Bugeranus carunculatus 139
Bulbul, Yellow-eared **92**
Bullfinch, Puerto Rico 151
Buphagus spp. 142
Burhinus vermiculatus 142
Bustards **33**, 36, 148
Butastur rufipennis 44
Buteo spp. 148
Butorides virescens 64
Buzzard, Grasshopper 44
Bycanistes brevis 30

Cairina moschata 141
Caloenas nicobarica 91, **92**
Camarhynchus pallidus **84**,
  85
Campylopterus
  phainopeplus 81
Capella stenura 105
Caprimulgus noctitherus
  150
Caracara **114**
Cassidix mexicanus 99
Cassowary, Double Wattled
  87
Casuarius casuarius 87
Cathartes aura 22
Centropelma micropterum 79
Centropus phasianinus 106,
  107
Centurus superciliaris 125
Certhidea olivacea 85
Ceryle rudis 69
Chalcomitra senegalensis
  101
Chiffchaff **109**
Chlidonias hybrida 61, 71
Chlorophoneus multicolor
  17
Chlorophonia, Blue-
  crowned **77**
Chloropsis spp. 113
Chloebia gouldiae 41
Chondrohierax uncinatus
  149
Circaetus gallicus 45
Circus maillardi maillardi
  148
Clytoceyx rex 18
Cochlearius cochlearius 64,
  71

Cockatoo, Black Palm 11
Cocks of the rock 27,
  26-27
Coereba flaveola **88**, 98
Collocalia francica **132**, 133
Columba vitiensis 91
Columbigallina talpacoti 99
Coots 79
Copsychus saularis 97, 125
Coragyps atratus 93
Cormorants **60**, 133
Corvus splendens 94
Cotinga, Black-necked Red
  23
Coucal 106, **107**
Coursers **36**, 37
Cowbird, Glossy 99
Crake, Ruddy **61**
Cranes **32**, 36, 46, 61, 139
Creatophora cinerea 113
Crow, House 94
Curassow, White-headed
  150

Dacelo novaeguineae **44**, 45
Darter **52**
Dendrocygna bicolor 69
Dicaeum cruentatum 97,
  118
Dikkop, Water 142
Diphyllodes magnificus 27
Dissowa episcopus 61
Doves **16**, 17, 99, **124**
Drepanoplectes jacksoni 46,
  47
Dromaius novaehollandiae
  34, **122**
Dromas ardeola 145
Ducks 57, 62, 66, 69, 79,
  140, 141, 146
Ducula spp. 11, 91

Eagles 22, 45, 54, 91, 115,
  123, 139, 152
Egrets **56**, 57, 71, 106, 128,
  129, 143
Egretta spp. **56**, 57, 128,
  129
Elanoides forficatus 22, 44
Emu 34, **122**
Erythrura prasina 119, **119**
Estrilda spp. 49, 106, 119,
  124
Ephippiorhynchus
  senegalensis 58
Eudocimus spp. 71, **70-71**,
  127

Euphoria, Golden-crowned **137**
Europyga helias 57, 113

Falco chicquera 114, **115**
Finchs 41, **84**, 85
Finch-bill, Laysan 151
Flamingos 70, **72**, 73, 78, **79**
Florican, Lesser 46
Flowerpeckers 83, **83**, 97, **118**
Flycatchers **9**, **19**, 63 101, **112**, 150
Forktail, Chestnut-naped **52**
Fulica spp. 79

Gallinago spp. 79
Gallus spp. 130, 140, **141**, 146
Geese 61, **61**, 62, **62**, 141, 155
Geospiza magnirostris **84**, 85
Gerygone magnirostris 63
Goshawk, African 123
Goura scheepmakeri 87
Grackles **92**, 99, **153**
Gracula religiosa intermedia 136
Grassquit, Glossy 40
Grebes 79, 153
Greenshank 58
Grenadier, Purple 49
Grus spp. 36, 46, 61
Guineafowl **32**, 36, **48**
Gypaetus barbatus meridionalis **152**, 153
Gypohierax angolensis 58-59
Gyps bengalensis 93, 94

Halcyon spp. 45
Haliaetus leucogaster 54
Haliastur indus 94
Hammerhead 69, 145
Harpia harpya 22, 139
Harrier, Reunion 148
Hawks 147, 148
Helmetbird 93
Helmet-crest, Bearded 80
Hemignathus lucidus 125
Hemiprocne longipennis **103**, 106
Herons **52**, 58-59, 61, **62** 64, 71
Heteronetta atricapilla 57
Hoatzin 57
Honeycreepers, Hawaiian

6-7, **6-7**, 85
Honeyeater, Cardinal **117**
Honeyguide, Black-throated **144**, 145
Hoplopterus spinosus 58
Hornbills 15, **15**, **20**, 30, **31**, **42**, 115, 130, 145
Hummingbirds **41**, 42, 53, 80, **80**, 81, 88, **89**, 109, **109**, 117
Hydranassa caerulea 71
Hydrophasianus chirurgus **68**, 72

Ibis leucocephalus 60
Ibises 61, 71, **70-71**, 127
Icterus nigrogularis 99
Indicator indicator **144**, 145
Irena puella 145

Jacamar, Paradise **19**
Jacanas 57, 68, **68**, 73, **73**
Junglefowl 130, 140, **141**, 146

Kagu 151
Kingfishers 18, 45, **52**, **59** **60**, 69, **69**
Kiskadee 29, 98, **98**
Kites 22, 44, 94, **114**, 149
Kookaburra 44, 45

Lammergeyer **152**, 153
Lanius collaris **100**, 101
Lark, Desert 38
Leafbird, Blue-winged **9**
Leistes militaris **104**, 106
Leptocoma jugularis 97
Leptoptilos spp. 94, **95**
Lophura spp. 25, **82**, 83, **154**, 155
Lorikeets **18**, **20**
Lorius roratus **16**, 17
Lovebird, Rosy-faced **42**
Loxigilla porficrosa grandis 151

Macaws 54, 135, **138**
Malacorhynchus membranaceus 62
Malcohas 91, **112**, 149, **149**
Mallard 141
Manacus vitellinus 27
Manakins **9**, 22, 27, **90**
Marshbirds **104**, 106
Megalaima haemacephala **9**, 97

Megalurus albolimbatus 63
Meleagris gallopavo 140
Melidora macrorhina 18
Mellisuga spp. 88
Merganetta armata 79
Merlin, Red-headed **114**, 115
Merops rubicus 44, **49**
Milvus miarans 94, **114**
Mimus polyglottos 99
Mockingbird 99
Molothrus bonariensis 99
Monarch, Black-naped Blue **90**
Moorhen, Lesser **59**
Mousebird, Speckled 100, **100**
Motmot, Blue-throated 76
Munia, Long-tailed 119, **119**
Myiagra ruficollis 63
Mynahs **124**, 125, 136, **137**

Nannopterum harrisi 85
Necrosyrtes monachus 94
Nectarinia fusca 42
Neophron percnopterus 93, **95**
Nettapus spp. 62
Nightjar, Pennant-winged **40**
Nukupuu 125

Oilbird 19, **75**
Opisthocomus hoazin 57
Oreotrochilus chimborazo 80
Orioles 83, 97, 99
Oriolus spp. 83, 97, 99
Oropendolas **28**, 29
Osprey 66
Ostrich 34, **35**, 39, 51, 128
Owl, Spotted Eagle **114**
Oxpeckers 142, **143**
Oxypogon guerinii 80

Pandion haliaetus 66
Paradisaea apoda 29, 126-127, **127**
Parakeets **43**, **92**, 122, 136
Parrots **10**, **16**, 17, 42, 54, 136, **137**, **151**, **154**
Partridge, Crested Green Wood 25
Passer domesticus **124**, 125-126
Pavo spp. 130, 141
Peafowl 24-25, **24**, 130, 141
Pedionomus torquatus 39
Pelecanus occidentalis 133

Pelican, Brown 133
Pezoporus wallicus 42
Phaenicophaeus pyrrhocephalus 149, **149**
Phalacrocorax bougainvillii 133
Phalarope, Red-necked **108**
Pharomachrus mocinno 76, **77**
Pheasants 25, **25**, **82**, 83, **154**, 155
Philepitta castanea 93
Phoeniconaias minor 70
Phoenicoparrus spp. 78, **79**
Phoenicopterus spp. **72**, 73, 78
Piapiac 142
Pigeons **18**, **20**, 29, 87, 91, **92**, **116**
Pitangus sulphuratus 98, **98**
Pithecophaga jefferyi 91, 152
Pitta baudi **82**, 83
granatina 25
Pittas 25, **82**, 83
Plains Wanderer 39
Plantaineater, Violet **10**
Platalea leucorodia 61
Plovers 58, **58**, **108**, 109, 142, 145
Pluvialis dominica **108**, 109
Pluvianus aegyptius 142
Podiceps spp. 79
Podilymbus gigas 153
Poicephalus spp. 42, 136
Poliospiza gularis 100
Pomarea nigra 150
Prionochilus xanthopygius 83, **83**
Probosciger aterrimus 11
Psilopogon pyrolophus 13
Psittacula spp. 122, 136
Psittacus erithacus 136
Psittirostra cantans 151
Ptilinopus spp. **16**, 17, 19
Ptilostomus afer 142

Quail, Harlequin **33**
Quelea, Red-billed **120**, 121
Quetzal 76, **77**

Rail, Chestnut **62**
Ramphocelus carbo 99, **99**
Ramphocinclus brachyurus 150

Raphus cucullatus 128
Recurvirostra avosetta 64, **65**
Redshank 58
Rhinoplax vigil 130
Rhodonessa caryophyllacea 146
Rhynochetus jubatus 151
Rockfowl 147, **147**
Robin, Magpie 97, 125
Roller, Lilac-breasted **42**
Rollulus roulroul 25
Rupicola spp. 27, **26-27**
Rynchops flavirostris 58-59

Sabrewing, Santa Marta 81
Sagittarius serpentarius 38
Sandgrouse 36, **36**, 39, 51
Sandpiper, Common 58, 142
Sarcoramphus papa 22
Scolopax rustica 111
Scopus umbretta 69, 145
Screamers 57
Scythebill **23**
Secretary Bird 38
Seedeaters 40, 100
Seedsnipe, Gay's 76
Shoebill 58-59, 64, 69
Shrikes 17, **100**, 101, **112**
Skimmer, African 58-59
Snipe **58**, 79, 105
Sparrows 41, **124**, 125-126, **137**
Spilornis cheela 115
Spizastur melaneleucus 22
Spoonbill, Roseate **67**
Sporophila americana 40
Spurfowl, Red-necked **33**
Starlings **96**, 113, 126
Steatornis caripensis 19, **75**
Storks 57, 58-59, 60, 61, 94
Struthio camelus 34, 35, 39, 51, 128
Sturnus vulgaris 125, **126**
Sula variegata 133
Sunbirds 41, 42, **96**, 97, 101, **101**, **151**
Swallow, House **109**
Swan, Black **63**
Swift, Crested Tree **103**, 106
Swiftlet, Grey-rumped **132**, 133
Sypheotides indica 46

Tanagers **23**, **98**, 99, **99**
Terns 61, 71, **108**
Terpsiphone viridis 101
Thrasher, White-breasted 150
Thraupis spp. **98**, 99
Threskiornis spp. 61, 71
Thrush, Bare-eyed 99
Tinamous **23**, 24
Tody, Jamaican **88**
Topaza pella 53
Toucans 14-15, **14**, **15**
Touraco, Knysna **116**
Tragopan blythi 146
Tragopans 146, **146**
Tringa spp. 58
Trochilus polytmus 88-89, **89**
Trogon, Whitehead's 83, **83**
Tropicranus albocristatus 145
Trumpeter, White-winged **56**
Turdus nudigenis 99
Turkeys 139, 140

Vanellus albiceps 58
Vanga curvirostris 93
Vanga, Hook-billed 93
Vidua fischeri 49
Vireo, Red-eyed **19**
Volatina jacarina 40
Vultures 22, 58-59, 93, 94, **95**

Warblers 63, 105
Waterhen, White-breasted 61, 105
Wattle-Eye, Yellow-bellied **112**
Waxbills 106, 119, **124**, **137**
Weaver, Village **101**
Whip-poor-will, Puerto Rico 150
White-eye, Oriental **90**
Whydahs 46, **47**, 49
Woodcock 111
Woodhewer **10**
Woodpeckers 12-13, **12**, **13**, 126

Zarhynchus wagleri 29
Zonaeginthus guttatus 41

TITLES IN THIS SERIES

Arts
Art Nouveau for Collectors/Collecting and Looking After
Antiques/Collecting Inexpensive Antiques/Silver for Collectors/
Toys and Dolls for Collectors

Domestic Animals and Pets
Cats/Dog Care/Dogs/Horses and Ponies/Tropical Freshwater
Aquaria/Tropical Marine Aquaria

Gardening
Flower Arranging/Garden Flowers/Garden Shrubs/House Plants

General Information
Aircraft/Beachcombing and Beachcraft/Espionage/Freshwater
Fishing/Modern Combat Aircraft/Modern First Aid/Photography/
Sailing/Sea Fishing/Trains/Wargames

History and Mythology
Witchcraft and Black Magic

Natural History
Bird Behaviour/Birds of Prey/Birdwatching/Butterflies/Fishes of the
World/Fossils and Fossil Collecting/A Guide to the Seashore/
Prehistoric Animals/Seabirds/Seashells/Trees of the World

Popular Science
Astrology/Astronomy/Biology/Computers at Work/Ecology/
Economics/Electricity/Electronics/Exploring the Planets/Geology/
The Human Body/Microscopes and Microscopic Life/Psychology/
Rocks, Minerals and Crystals/The Weather Guide